Promoting positive behaviour supporting people with a learning disability and people with autism

Series Editor: Lesley Barcham

Mandatory unit and Common Induction Standards titles

Communicating effectively with people with a learning disability
ISBN 978 0 85725 510 5

Personal development for learning disability workers ISBN 978 0 85725 609 6

Equality and inclusion for learning disability workers ISBN 978 0 85725 514 3

Duty of care for learning disability workers ISBN 978 0 85725 613 3

Principles of safeguarding and protection for learning disability workers
ISBN 978 0 85725 506 8

Person centred approaches when supporting people with a learning disability
ISBN 978 0 85725 625 6

The role of the learning disability worker ISBN 978 0 85725 637 9

Handling information for learning disability workers ISBN 978 0 85725 633 1

Titles supporting a unit from the level 2 health and social care qualifications

An introduction to supporting people with autistic spectrum conditions
ISBN 978 0 85725 710 7

An introduction to supporting people with a learning disability
ISBN 978 0 85725 709 3

Titles supporting a unit from the level 3 health and social care qualifications

Promoting positive behaviour when supporting people with a learning
disability and people with autism ISBN 978 0 85725 713 0

Promoting positive behaviour when supporting people with a learning disability and people with autism

Sharon Paley

Supporting a unit from the level 3 health
and social care qualifications

Los Angeles | London | New Delhi
Singapore | Washington DC

all about people

Learning Matters
An imprint of SAGE Publications Ltd
1 Oliver's Yard
55 City Road
London EC1Y 1SP

SAGE Publications Inc.
2455 Teller Road
Thousand Oaks, California 91320

SAGE Publications India Pvt Ltd
B 1/I 1 Mohan Cooperative Industrial Area
Mathura Road
New Delhi 110 044

SAGE Publications Asia-Pacific Pte Ltd
3 Church Street
#10–04 Samsung Hub
Singapore 049483

Editor: Luke Block
Production controller: Chris Marke
Project management: Deer Park Productions
Marketing manager: Tamara Navaratnam
Cover design: Pentacor
Typeset by: Pantek Media, Maidstone, Kent
Printed by: Ashford Colour Printers Ltd, Gosport, Hants

BILD
Campion House
Green Street
Kidderminster
Worcestershire
DY10 1JL
© 2012 BILD

First published in 2012 jointly by Learning Matters Ltd
and the British Institute of Learning Disabilities.

British Library Cataloguing in Publication Data

A catalogue record for this book is available from the
British Library

ISBN 978 0 85725 713 0
ISBN 978 0 85725 852 6 (hbk)

Contents

This book covers:

- The Level 3 health and social care unit HSC 3045 – Promote positive behaviour

Acknowledgements

Photographs from www.crocstockimages.com, www.careimages.com, www.thepowerofpositiveimages.com and Photosymbols.

Our thanks to Sophie, Choices Housing and Autism Plus for their help.

About the author

Sharon Paley

Sharon Paley is a nurse for people with learning disabilities. She started her career as a nursery nurse, working with young children with severe learning disabilities. Sharon has spent most of her career working in services that support people who may be described as challenging. Sharon has extensive experience of working in community settings and of supporting people with a forensic history.

Sharon is the development manager for positive behaviour support at BILD. She has worked for BILD since 1998, taking on a number of different roles and responsibilities in that time. Sharon is also the director of a small training and consultancy company that specialises in delivering training to develop individual positive behaviour support packages for people who have learning disabilities and autism.

She also provides expert advice to the courts in England, including the Court of Protection.

Introduction

Who is this book for?

Promoting Positive Behaviour when Supporting People with a Learning Disability and People with Autism will provide the foundation if you:

- want a comprehensive introduction to promoting positive behaviour;

- work in health or social care, supporting people with a learning disability and/or people with autism and want to work to promote positive behaviour;

- are a manager in a service supporting people whose behaviour sometimes challenges and you have training or supervisory responsibility for the development of your colleagues;

- are a direct payment or personal budget user and are planning learning opportunities for your personal assistant.

Several other books in this series will help you gain a fuller understanding of how to provide good support to people whose behaviour is seen as challenging, including:

- *An Introduction to Supporting People with a Learning Disability;*

- *Next Steps in Supporting People with Autistic Spectrum Conditions;*

- *Communicating Effectively with People with a Learning Disability;*

- *Person Centred Approaches when Supporting People with a Learning Disability;*

- *Handling Information for Learning Disability Workers.*

Links to qualifications

This book gives you all of the information you need to complete the level 3 unit, *Promote positive behaviour*, from the level 3 diploma in health and social care and the level 3 learning disability certificates and award. You may use the learning from this book to:

- work towards a full qualification, for example the level 3 diploma in health and social care or a level 3 certificate or award;

- achieve accreditation for a single unit on promoting positive behaviour.

Although anyone studying for the qualifications will find the book useful, it is particularly helpful for people who provide services to or who support people with a learning disability or people with autism. The stories and examples used in this book are provided by people with a learning disability and people with an autistic spectrum condition, family carers and people working with them.

Links to assessment

If you are studying for this unit and want to gain accreditation towards a qualification, first of all you will need to make sure that you are registered with an awarding organisation which offers the qualification. Then you will need to provide a portfolio of evidence for assessment. The person responsible for training within your organisation will advise you about registering with an awarding organisation and give you information about the type of evidence you will need to provide for assessment. You can also get additional information from BILD. For more information about qualifications and assessment, please go to the BILD website: www.bild.org/qualifications

How this book is organised

Each chapter covers one learning outcome from the qualification unit *Promote positive behaviour*. The learning outcomes covered are clearly highlighted at the beginning of each chapter. Each chapter starts with a story from a person with a learning disability, a person with autism, a family carer or a worker. This introduces the topic and is intended to help you think about the issues from their point of view. Each chapter contains:

Thinking points – to help you reflect on your practice;

Stories – examples of good support from people with learning disabilities and people with autism and family carers;

Activities – for you to use to help you to think about your work and how you offer support;

Key points – a summary of the main messages in that chapter;

References and where to go for more information – useful references to help further study.

At the end of the book there is:

A glossary – explaining any jargon or specialist language in plain English;

An index – to help you look up a particular topic easily.

Study skills

Studying for a qualification can be very rewarding. However, it can be daunting if you have not studied for a long time, or are wondering how to fit your studies into an already busy life. The BILD website contains lots of advice to help you to study successfully, including information about effective reading, taking notes, organising your time and using the internet for research. For further information, go to www.bild.org/qualifications

Chapter 1
Promoting positive behaviour support

For the sake of a plate of chips

Herbert liked chips; he hated curry, chilli and stews. He liked chips, preferably with sausages.

Herbert had lived at home until he was 50. Following the death of his father, his elderly mother found it difficult to cope with supporting Herbert. He was grieving and he became aggressive towards his mother, blaming her for his father's death.

Eventually it was decided that Herbert should have a short break and he went to stay for a few weeks in a small residential home, close to where he lived with his mother. The team supporting Herbert liked him a lot, but he was very aggressive at meal times when he always wanted chips, chips and more chips. Eventually this came to a head when Herbert smashed the TV after he was refused chips.

'Why is he doing this? What's the matter? We can't just give into him, he'll learn that behaving badly is how you get what you want,' said one team member. 'I agree, and anyway chips are bad for you,' replied a second team member.

'Herbert is grieving, he's lost his father, he's now separated from his mother and perhaps chips are all he's got left,' said another team member. They all sat in silence. 'Surely, for the sake of a few oven chips we can calm this situation and Herbert can have some control over his life again.'

Herbert's behaviour was caused by a number of factors and he wasn't really angry about dinner. In fact, he was angry that he had lost the life he knew and the chips were just a symbol of his past life and how he recognised his 'world order'. It was a tangible way for Herbert to assert control and communicate his own needs.

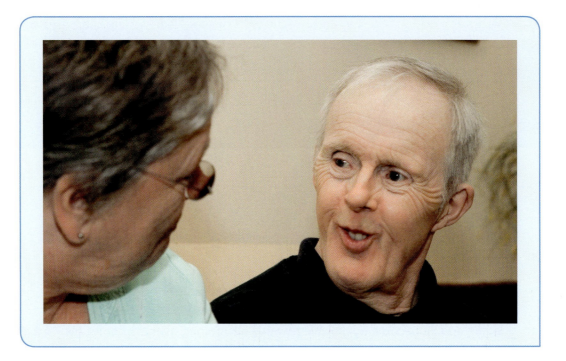

Introduction

This chapter explores some of the knowledge and skills you will need to promote positive behaviour. This includes understanding the factors that may be associated with or contribute to behaviour that is seen as challenging, the use of proactive strategies, the reinforcement of positive behaviours and ways to model good practice. The chapter starts with an explanation of the language used in this book.

It is important to understand and remember that whilst most human behaviour is appropriate when exhibited in certain settings, it is often the setting, the risk or other people's reaction to a behaviour which will mean it is considered to be 'challenging'.

When you take action to try to prevent any challenging behaviour occurring before it happens, then you are behaving in a proactive way. When you are supporting a person with a learning disability or a person with autism and you understand some of the factors that might lead to their behaviour being seen as challenging, then proactive plans can be put in place that might prevent such incidents occurring.

This chapter identifies and explores proactive strategies before moving on to look in more detail at how praise and supporting the positive aspects of a person's behaviour can lead to positive changes and responses. It concludes by looking at ways in which you can work with others to understand and model good practice in promoting positive behaviour.

Learning outcomes

This chapter will help you to:

- understand the language used in this book;
- explain what factors may cause or be associated with 'challenging behaviour';
- assess the effectiveness of proactive strategies on lessening the incidence of challenging behaviour;
- explain how praise and supporting the positive aspects of an individual's behaviour can reinforce positive behaviour;
- demonstrate how to model best practice in promoting positive behaviour to colleagues and others.

This chapter covers:

Level 3 HSC 3045 – Promote positive behaviour: Learning Outcome 3

A word about language

This book is about providing good support for people with a learning disability and for people with autism, in particular for people whose behaviour is seen to challenge services. In the fields of learning disability and autism, the language we use is changing and developing all the time. This is as a result of listening to people's personal experience, of changing values and attitudes in society and of new research. In addition, the use of language varies from country to country.

In the UK, the term 'learning disability' is a label widely used when describing an impairment that starts before adulthood and has a lasting effect on a person's development. It includes the presence of a significantly reduced ability to understand new or complex information or to learn new skills. It also means having a reduced ability to cope independently. In other countries (for example Canada, Australia, New Zealand and the USA) the term 'intellectual disability' is often used to describe the same kind of impairment.

The language used to describe the autistic spectrum has also developed and changed over time. In this book we use the term autistic spectrum conditions

(ASC), which is one of several in common usage at the time of writing. Autistic spectrum disorder is still used in more clinical and research settings. The term 'autism' is also in common usage and is still widely accepted as an umbrella term for the spectrum, for example by the National Autistic Society. In this book we use 'autistic spectrum conditions' as it is a more neutral and less medical term than 'autistic spectrum disorder'.

You can find out more about the terms learning disability and autism in the books *An Introduction to Supporting People with Autistic Spectrum Conditions* and *An Introduction to Supporting People with a Learning Disability* in this series.

In this book you will frequently see the terms positive behaviour support and challenging behaviour. Positive behaviour support is an approach that promotes the individuality, rights and dignity of the person. Positive behaviour support is based on the person centred principles of encouraging independence, developing and sustaining relationships, personalised support and positive communication. Positive behaviour support seeks to achieve change for the person by supporting them to develop alternatives to the behaviours which present a risk to the person or to others. The approach aims to reduce the use of restrictive interventions and is based on evidence which promotes behavioural assessment and interventions and lifestyle changes that aim to enhance the quality of life of the person.

In this book when the term 'challenging behaviour' is used it is to describe a particular behaviour and the impact that behaviour might have on the individual or others: it should not be applied to an individual. The behaviour may affect the person's health; it may present short or long term risks to their safety or the safety of others; or it may be culturally or socially unacceptable. Behaviours that impact on the quality of the person's life, their physical or mental health may be described as challenging. The presence of behaviours that challenge will impact on the life experiences of the person.

Factors that may be associated with behaviours which are challenging

Behaviour may be described as 'challenging' for a variety of reasons, for example because:

- other people find the behaviour difficult to manage or understand;
- the behaviour presents a risk to the person, their friends and family or other people who spend time with them;

- the behaviour is not appropriate for the environment in which it is being exhibited;
- the behaviour is not appropriate when thinking about the person's age and abilities.

A person may behave in 'challenging ways' for many reasons. If you are to work to promote appropriate alternative behaviour, then it is important that you try to understand why the person presents such behaviour. Understanding the factors that contribute to a person's behaviour will help you to provide good support and to decide what can be done to help the person behave differently.

When you are faced with challenging behaviour, it is always tempting to look for 'the cause'. If only 'the cause' can be found, then everything will be all right. This can be true sometimes, but there is very rarely a single cause for a person's behaviour. The cause of any behaviour is usually made up of many different factors. So it is unlikely you will find a *single* cause of a person's behaviour.

Therefore, it is more helpful to seek to understand the different factors influencing a person's behaviour. Although you may not find all of the factors that come together to cause a particular behaviour, you may be able to identify a sufficient number. Even if you are unable to change a person's behaviour, the knowledge of why the behaviour occurs can be reassuring and helpful to those who support them and care about them.

Personal and environmental factors that might influence behaviour

As previously discussed, our behaviour is the result of a number of different factors; these can be split into the two broad categories of personal and environmental. This division helps us to think about the factors in relation to what is going on inside the person and what is going on around them. The table overleaf gives some examples of personal and environmental factors that might contribute towards a person's behaviour being seen as challenging.

Personal factors that might influence a person's behaviour

Constitution – This refers to the person's physical state, for example do they have any allergies, chronic illnesses or a sensory impairment? It includes any mental health needs the person is experiencing and also whether any drugs they are taking might be affecting their behaviour. Is the person in pain and unable to explain this? Under this heading, think about any syndrome, disorder or condition the person may have and its impact on their behaviour.

Personality and character – Is the person an extrovert or introvert, moody or laid back, easily aroused and frustrated or quiet and withdrawn? How does their personality affect their behaviour? Do they have a 'bad reputation' that may not be justified?

Sense of self – Does the person have a positive or negative self image? Low or high self esteem? How much self knowledge does the person have? Are their cultural and religious needs understood and addressed?

Communication skills – This includes the person's ability to understand and act on the communication of others and to communicate their own thoughts, feelings and needs to those they are with. Can the person hear and see clearly the verbal and non verbal communication of others? Are their language and cultural needs understood and being addressed?

Environmental factors that may influence a person's behaviour

The quality of the physical environment – This includes lighting, noise, amount of personal space, heat, humidity, colour, smells, etc.

The quality of the social environment – Is the person bored and under stimulated? Or is it too busy with too many other people? What is the quality of the person's relationships? Are the key people in their life hostile and cold or emotionally close and supportive? Does the person have a chance to spend time with the important people in their life such as family or friends? Is the person lonely?

Power and choice – Can the person make choices in their daily life? Or do they have very little control? Is the person supported to make choices? Do the people supporting the person stress conformity and make them comply with their wishes? Or are the person's choices and decisions respected and acted on? Is there access to advocacy support?

Unpredictable occurrences – Is the person startled or unsure about what is happening to them and in their environment? Do events happen to the person without them being prepared or without considering their needs and wishes? Can the person influence their daily routine?

Psychological state – Has the person recently experienced any changes, loss or bereavement in their life? Has he or she been a victim of abuse (sexual, physical, hate crime, etc)? Is the person anxious, lonely or feeling excluded?

Other people's communication – Do the people in day to day contact with the person communicate well or poorly? Do they use words and non verbal communication that are too complex and difficult? Does communication often break down between the person and their main supporters?

Incentives and negative consequences – Is the person getting positive rewards (incentives) as a result of a particular behaviour? Or is the person experiencing negative consequences?

Personal factors help to explain why different people behave differently even when apparently in the same situation and seemingly having the same experiences. Environmental factors will help you to explore some of the things you might be able to change. These help to explain why challenging behaviours sometimes increase or decrease following any changes in where a person lives, or how they spend their days, or when the people who support them change.

The interaction of personal and environmental factors

It can often be the case that personal and environmental factors combine to cause a person to behave in challenging ways. For example, if a person has difficulty in speaking due to their disability then this is a personal factor. However, if other people have difficulty in understanding them then this is an external factor which might make the situation worse. When both of these factors come together, it may lead to the person feeling frustrated or ignored and the person might then behave in a challenging way in order to get people to listen or take notice of them.

When working with a person with a particular syndrome or condition, you and your colleagues will need to have a full understanding of its possible effect on behaviour. For example, a person with autism and a learning disability may present behaviour that their family members and support workers find difficult to understand and that they believe to be challenging. Once you can understand how the person's autism affects them and their behaviour, you will be better equipped to know what to do and how to prevent specific responses on other occasions. It is easier to understand a person's behaviour if you have a better understanding of their experiences: this may include considering how having an autistic spectrum condition has affected their communication, social interactions, rigidity of thought and their sensory awareness.

This doesn't mean that environmental factors are not important – they are often the trigger for particular behaviours. However, a better knowledge of a syndrome or condition might help you to gain a deeper understanding of a person's behaviour and its possible function.

What happens in the environment around the person is often under the control of the people supporting them. It is important to recognise that everyone offering support has the power to change the environment in ways that are often not available to the person being supported. For example, if you know that a person you support finds being with lots of people in a small room difficult, then you can reduce the impact of this simply by ensuring that the person does not spend time in confined spaces with lots of people. Don't forget, in most cases, personal and environmental factors interact and this can increase the risk of behaviour that challenges being exhibited.

Activity

Think about a person that you have supported in the past or someone you support now. Can you identify any possible factors that may contribute to them using behaviour that is difficult for people to understand and manage or which may cause harm to themselves or other people?

Discuss your ideas with a more experienced colleague or your manager and find out from them what they think are the main factors that contribute to the person's behaviour.

Improving communication

Communication difficulties can often create problems for people with a learning disability and for people with autistic spectrum conditions. Communication breakdown may contribute to challenging behaviour. It is important to understand each person's individual communication and work to better understand what they are trying to convey.

All communication has three parts to it:

1. **Verbal messages** – the words we use.

2. **Paraverbal messages** – how we say the words, sometimes called intonation.

3. **Non verbal messages** – our body language or behaviour.

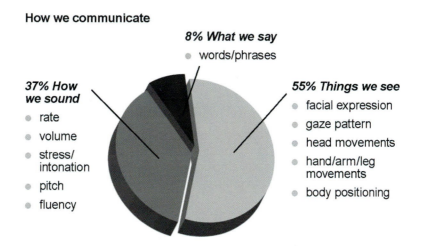

How we communicate

8% What we say
- words/phrases

37% How we sound
- rate
- volume
- stress/intonation
- pitch
- fluency

55% Things we see
- facial expression
- gaze pattern
- head movements
- hand/arm/leg movements
- body positioning

Knowing that only eight per cent of our communication is verbal is important when thinking about its impact on behaviour, as this means that many people with a learning disability or people with autism will have real difficulties in picking up non verbal cues. Most people have an expectation that there will be consistency between our spoken communication, tone of voice and behaviour. People who have a learning disability or people with autism may not have the ability to communicate in such complex ways; this could then lead to a lack of understanding between the person and those who are supporting them. A breakdown in communication with a person you support can result in the following feelings.

- **Frustration** – because the person is unable to influence what is happening to them or other people's behaviour. People with poor communication skills can become passive because they are always on the receiving end of other people's actions or decision making. In addition, they may become frustrated and angry because of their lack of power in influencing their environment.

- **Isolation** – many people who are difficult to understand get less attention from other people including those employed to support them. As a result, they have fewer opportunities to develop close relationships and less incentive for getting on with people. It is very important that the issues of communication are addressed. Everyone offering support needs to develop consistent and clear ways of building positive relationships that address issues of likes, dislikes, preferences, choices and decision making.

There is more information about communicating with people with a learning disability and people with autism in the books *Communicating Effectively with People with a Learning Disability* and *An Introduction to Supporting People with Autistic Spectrum Conditions*, which are part of this series.

Helping people to communicate can be very important in supporting them to express themselves as an alternative to using challenging behaviour. You may find it useful to consider these questions:

- How much does a person really understand? Some people may use and appear to understand words that they do not really understand.

- Does the person get chances to talk to other people or express their views and opinions?

- Can you find a range of different ways to help a person communicate?

- Can the person make choices for themselves and are there ways to improve how a person can take part in personal decision making?

- Is the right support available to ensure that each person understands what is happening to them and uses their chosen means of communication to be involved?

- Have you found out how a person communicates by asking their family, friends or people who know them well?

It is important to understand each person's individual communication and work to better understand what they are trying to convey.

Understanding positive incentives and negative consequences

We all behave in certain ways because we have learnt that this works for us. For example, if we are hungry we might make a sandwich or if we are tired we go to bed. These provide a fairly direct and instant positive incentive or reward. Other incentives may be more subtle. If you like the company of others, you learn to be friendly and sociable. The positive incentive or motivator for this behaviour is that people find you good company and enjoy spending time with you.

However, not all behaviour results in a positive incentive or reward. In fact, some behaviours produce the opposite outcome and result in a negative consequence.

If you like driving fast but get several speeding fines or a driving ban, then the financial cost of the penalty fines and the cost and inconvenience of the ban could be powerful negative consequences which result in you driving more slowly.

Behaviours which are followed by a positive incentive (or a reinforcing event) are more likely to happen again in the future, whereas those which are followed by a negative consequence (or a penalty) are not. Clearly, for people with a learning disability and autism, support should aim to provide positive incentives for the desired behaviour. However, when people present behaviour that is seen as challenging you should identify whether there are any positive incentives which are making the behaviour rewarding.

When we gain something from a behaviour, this can increase the likelihood of that behaviour occurring. We will then persist in behaving that way, sometimes for a long period of time even when we recognise that such behaviour may be bad for us or our health. If such behaviour becomes an integral part of our personal identity and how we relate to other people, then it will be much harder for us to stop.

People may behave in a certain way because it:

- helps them to experience nice feelings – perhaps the behaviour enables the person to feel happy or experience feelings that they find enjoyable;

- helps them to avoid sensations – it may be that the environment is too noisy, too hot or too cold and that the behaviour enables them to escape or move away;

- means they can avoid activities – the person may either dislike the task or find it difficult and use a certain behaviour for avoidance;

- stops them going into crowded places or being with other people – social avoidance can be quite common in very young children or children who have developmental delay. Activities that require co-operation with others may be difficult for some people so they may use a behaviour to avoid such situations;

- may help them to get things – the person knows that the behaviour will help them to obtain 'a tangible reward'. It may be something they can use or something they particularly like, for example the opportunity to read a book or watch a DVD;

- is an opportunity to interact and communicate with other people – a person may be using their behaviour to communicate an unmet need. It may simply be that they like engaging with other people.

Understanding the positive incentives and natural negative consequences of particular behaviours is important when seeking to understand the factors behind a person's behaviour. You will find more information about this in Chapter 2.

Evaluating the effectiveness of proactive strategies

Understanding proactive strategies

Much of your work in supporting people with a learning disability or people with autism needs to focus on making positively valued and socially appropriate behaviour worthwhile. This can be achieved by positive approaches so that you can improve communication with the person and build fulfilling relationships. The good practice approach outlined in this book sets out how to take a proactive approach to support people to develop socially appropriate and worthwhile behaviours. More information on developing proactive and reactive strategies and approaches can be found in Chapter 2.

It is important to work with the person you support in proactive ways. This can be done by:

- working in person centred ways and recognising the importance of responding to the person, what they want and like in meeting their needs;

- identifying what the person is good at or what they enjoy doing and supporting them to do this more often;

- involving the person, their relatives and friends in their support planning;

- understanding the needs of the person;

- supporting the person to be as independent as possible;

- helping the person to keep physically and mentally well;

- supporting the person to experience a range of friendships and relationships;

- helping the person to have a fulfilling life;

- offering encouragement to the person whenever possible;

- praising them when they are being positive and interacting well with other people;

- telling the person when they are doing well, this is called positive feedback.

How can you evaluate the effectiveness of proactive approaches?

Examples of proactive approaches include the following:

- Ensure the person gets 'what they want' through socially appropriate behaviours.

  For example, Naomi enjoys having a bath and needs to feel clean all the time. However, she will strip naked if she feels she has got too dirty. A proactive approach to supporting Naomi and managing this behaviour would be to offer her baths and other ways of keeping clean more frequently so that she doesn't need to strip in order to get a bath.

- Avoid exposure to external factors which may 'trigger' the behaviour which causes concern.

  Mohammed is autistic and he doesn't like crowded environments as he finds the sensory experience too overwhelming. Crowded places make him very distressed and he sometimes self injures in crowded shops in order to get away from the cause of his distress. However, Mohammed enjoys shopping for his own clothes and for presents for other people. A proactive approach to supporting Mohammed would be to plan to help him to do his Christmas shopping in late November or in the early morning when the shops are less crowded. Alternatively, Mohammed could be supported to shop at small independent high street shops which may be less crowded. Consideration should be given to doing his shopping over several short trips rather than one long shopping outing.

- Ensure the person receives sensory stimulation in a way that doesn't cause them harm.

  Stephen enjoys sensory stimulation and will bounce around his home, occasionally bumping into people or banging into walls hurting himself or damaging furniture. Staff are now supporting Stephen to enjoy positive sensory activities such as horse riding, swimming, cycling, or bouncing on a trampoline to reduce the sensory seeking behaviours which are more risky when they occur indoors.

When you implement proactive approaches to reduce behaviours which are viewed as challenging, it is important to evaluate them to ensure that:

- the approach can be implemented with consistency by all involved in the person's life;
- there is evidence to show the approach is appropriate and effective;
- the approach is effective in reducing the frequency of the behaviour you are concerned with;
- the strategy is effective in reducing the intensity of the behaviour of concern;
- the level of risk associated with the behaviour is reducing.

There are a number of ways that you can evaluate a proactive strategy, including the following:

1. Use reports and records to establish how often the behaviour occurs prior to implementing a proactive strategy (this is called establishing a baseline for the behaviour). Compare the frequency of the behaviour after the proactive approach has been implemented. You would hope to see a reduction in the frequency of the behaviour over time.

2. Analyse data to see if the team is applying the strategy consistently. If the behaviour of concern does occur, then explore what was happening at the time, who was supporting the person and which strategy had been implemented to prevent the behaviour of concern emerging.

3. All the people who are involved in supporting the person should meet on a regular basis to ensure they have analysed all of the information to hand and to discuss progress. They can also ensure that all of the information is being captured.

4. Review risk assessments on a regular basis. This could be as frequently as weekly if you are working to reduce high risk behaviour. Analyse the data to ensure there is a reduction in the actual risk.

Continually review and reflect on what is happening and then adapt the strategy as progress is made. This will support the team to continue with their proactive approaches and ensure that everyone is kept involved. Ensure that all progress is noted and that the whole team recognises the improvements. Remember, progress can often be slow at first and you are likely to experience an increase in the frequency of the behaviour of concern in the first week or two that a new approach is tried. Consistency will achieve positive behavioural change over time. There is more information on reviewing and revising approaches to promoting positive behaviour in Chapter 5.

You will know when a proactive approach has worked when:

- there is a change in the behaviour of concern, although it may initially become more frequent before decreasing in frequency;
- the team feels more confident and learns to deliver well targeted support with consistency;
- data can be used more effectively to review the behaviour of concern;
- assessed risk associated with the behaviour decreases;
- staff perceptions of the behaviours exhibited by the person appear to be more positive;
- the person spends more time engaged in positive activities and enjoys an increase in opportunities;
- the person's general health appears to improve;
- the person is less frequently exposed to the use of restrictive practices, such as physical interventions.

Tina is 26 and has autism and a severe learning disability. Tina enjoys lots of activities such as singing, using the sensory room and swimming. When Tina is at home, she enjoys watching DVDs of motor sport and will spend up to two hours a day watching these DVDs. It can be very difficult to get Tina to stop watching a DVD and take part in any alternative activity. Recently she has become more withdrawn and is increasing the time she spends watching the DVDs. Last night, when it was time for tea, she refused to eat and then became very distressed when staff tried to encourage her to turn the DVD off. The staff reported that Tina started to self injure, pulling her hair and banging her head with clenched fists and making the top of her right ear bleed.

This is a new behaviour to her support team, although records indicate that Tina did previously self injure. However, the last occasion was six years ago when she was at residential college. The cause then was thought to be related to hormonal changes.

Think about how proactive approaches may reduce the circumstances which lead to Tina being distressed and exhibiting self injurious behaviour. Are there any alternative strategies which could be employed to decrease the trigger events?

What do you think you should do immediately to manage the risks associated with the 'new' behaviour of self injury?

How can a proactive approach be implemented by her staff team?

How will you evaluate the strategies that the team implement?

Reinforcing positive behaviour

Positive reinforcement techniques such as praise, encouragement and giving positive feedback promote non challenging behaviour and support people to form positive relationships.

Think of a person who has had a positive impact on you and made you believe you could do something you would otherwise have believed was impossible for you to achieve. What did they do that made a difference? Did they do any of the following?

- *Take an interest in the things which were of interest to you?*
- *Give you encouragement?*
- *Help you learn a new skill?*
- *Introduce you to a new interest?*
- *Inspire you?*

Most of all, it is likely that they encouraged you, said positive things to you, reinforced your positive behaviours and acknowledged your achievements, no matter how small they were. This person understood you and took time to support you as another human.

Positive reinforcement is really very simple – we reinforce the positive behaviours and qualities that people express. This doesn't mean that you ignore behaviours which are risky or cause concern. Instead, the emphasis is on not highlighting them as 'problem' behaviours, but in trying to work in positive and proactive ways so as to reduce the impact these behaviours may have on the person.

Take time to think about how you could apply these principles in your day to day work when supporting someone who is at risk due to exhibiting behaviours described as challenging. Helping people to develop feelings of positive self worth can be a great antidote to 'challenging behaviour'. Examples of positive opportunities and praise include the following:

- **New experiences**: some people change positively when trying new activities, learning new skills and feeling a sense of achievement. Remember this will need to be assessed and managed carefully for each individual, as some people may feel stressed by new opportunities. This may be especially true for some people who have autism.

- **Choice and control**: supporting the person to take control over their life and develop the ability to make informed choices. Positive interactions create the opportunity to increase the skills people need to be able to make choices and communicate effectively.

- **Relationships**: supporting the person to maintain and develop important relationships will increase the person's sense of emotional wellbeing.

- **Supporting emotional expression**: we have already discussed behaviour as a means of communication. Supporting people to develop ways in which they can communicate how they are feeling could actually lead to a decrease in reliance on 'challenging behaviour'.

For people with a learning disability and people with autism, support should always aim to provide a positive experience for appropriate behaviour. As well as looking for the positive incentives for certain behaviours, it is important to remember the power of positive verbal reinforcement. We all like to be recognised for something we have achieved, to be thanked or praised for a job well done, or encouraged for our attempts. Providing praise and giving positive feedback can help to promote non challenging behaviour. In turn, this can lead to chances for better communication and more positive relationships.

It is important that we consider how we interact with people who exhibit behaviours we perceive to be challenging to us. Are people viewed as 'problematic' and are they expected to 'fit in' with how the service is being delivered? Are people expected to conform to the service or is the service adapted and delivered to meet the needs of each individual?

Modelling best practice in promoting positive behaviour

It is important, when you are working together with colleagues, family carers and other professionals to support a person with their behaviour, that you all provide support in the same way. This is called consistency. It is important to be consistent when supporting people who may exhibit some behaviour we find challenging as this will help to create structure and reduce stress for them.

You can achieve consistency by having a good person centred plan and a clear and detailed daily care or support plan that everyone knows about and follows. This will mean that people need to know what, when and how to provide the right support and the team will have to share their knowledge to make sure that the plan can be put in place by everyone. If all involved listen and learn from each other and share their skills and knowledge, then this will help to support the person to achieve their goals and enjoy a life that is appropriate to their needs.

When new members join the team they will look to more experienced team members for guidance. It is important to be a positive role model when supporting people who may behave in challenging ways. New team members may be apprehensive, thinking that a person doesn't like them or is trying to hurt them. You can help by:

- being positive;
- making sure that you are approachable by being friendly and open;
- making sure that you know about and understand each person's support plan and methods of communication;

- being a good role model and communicating with everyone in positive ways;
- ensuring that you have a consistent approach;
- being aware of your own limitations;
- working as a team member to ensure that the agreed policy, guidance and plans are acted upon;
- thinking about your own behaviour and how others may view it.

As an experienced member of the support team, you will have a lot to offer new team members as a good role model.

Practical ways in which you can model good practice

1. **Try to understand why the person may use a particular type of behaviour:** this is often the first step to supporting a person to use a behaviour less.

2. **Establish good relationships with the person:** try and learn how the person communicates. Recognise their emotional states and respond to them appropriately.

3. **Encourage positive interactions:** when the person shows behaviours that are not challenging and that are socially appropriate, you should use these as opportunities to encourage them.

4. **Encourage participation:** support the person to do more of the things they enjoy. The busier people are, doing the things they enjoy, the less likely they are to resort to behaviours that challenge.

5. **Establish good relationships with family and friends:** support the person to maintain their relationships with family and friends and take time to learn from them about the person, their ways of communicating and history.

Activity

Go back and reread the story about Herbert at the beginning of this chapter. Imagine that you are a member of staff in the small residential home supporting him. Write down:

- *how you would find out about the personal and environmental factors that might be influencing his behaviour;*
- *two proactive strategies that you might put in place to encourage positive behaviour;*
- *two ways that you might reinforce positive behaviour.*

Discuss your ideas with your line manager or an experienced colleague.

Key points from this chapter

- Knowing a person well and understanding their history is important.

- Many different factors can contribute to a person's behaviour being seen as challenging.

- Personal factors that might influence a person's behaviour include the person's health, personality and character, their communication skills and psychological state.

- Environmental factors that might influence a person's behaviour include the quality of the person's physical and social environment, the amount of choice and control they have in their life, other people's communication with them and any positive incentives or negative consequences they experience as a result of their behaviour.

- It is important to consider why a person uses a particular behaviour. Is it primarily a form of communication especially if the person has communication difficulties?

- Consider how you can support the person to take control of their life by enabling choice and decision making.

- Think about how positive life experiences can be supported for the individual and create new opportunities.

- Support the person to get what they would like from their life in ways other than using a behaviour which is risky to them or others.

- Help the person to improve their relationships by trying to understand them better, improving their opportunities for positive communication and encouraging opportunities to be meaningfully engaged.

- Positive reinforcement techniques such as praise, encouragement and giving positive feedback promote non challenging behaviours and support people in forming positive relationships.

References and where to go for more information

References

Hatton, S and Boughton, T (2011) *An Introduction to Supporting People with Autistic Spectrum Conditions.* Exeter: Learning Matters/BILD

Hardie, E and Tilly, L (2011) *An Introduction to Supporting People with a Learning Disability.* Exeter: Learning Matters/BILD

Thurman, S (2011) *Communicating Effectively with People with a Learning Disability.* Exeter: Learning Matters/BILD

Websites

BILD www.bild.org.uk

Challenging Behaviour Foundation www.thecbf.org.uk

National Autistic Society www.autism.org.uk

Chapter 2

Understanding proactive and reactive strategies

Meera has always found mornings difficult. But recently she has been getting very irritable when she is woken up too early. She will shout and swear at the person going into her room and has recently started to kick people and has even spat at one person when they entered her room to help her get up. The workers supporting Meera recognise that if they talk too much, or put music on her radio, this increases her level of upset and the behaviours which cause concern.

Meera's twin sister, Asya, who lives in the same house, has started to get up very early and she likes to play her music loudly. She also shouts quite a lot if she's left alone, which seems to affect Meera as well.

At the staff meeting the manager, Rita, asks all the support team for their ideas. Why might Asya be waking so much earlier most mornings and why is Meera finding the mornings so difficult? The team explores the possible factors influencing these behaviours and how they can manage the situation positively for both Meera and Asya.

Introduction

The story above shows why it is important for the team supporting a person whose behaviour is seen as challenging to think and work in proactive ways. Being proactive means getting to know the person well and supporting them in a person centred way. It means focusing on the person's needs, the factors that contribute to their behaviours, but also on their long term hopes, dreams and aspirations. It is often too easy to be reactive and respond to the immediate situation focusing on reducing the current risks. This can lead to forgetting about the long term aspirations a person may have and their overall physical and mental wellbeing.

This chapter explains the possible proactive and reactive strategies that can be used when supporting a person with a learning disability or a person with autism in relation to behaviours that can be seen as challenging. It looks at how to identify possible triggers for challenging behaviour as well as the importance of maintaining a person centred approach.

The chapter concludes by explaining the importance of reinforcing positive behaviour and describes the impact on an individual's wellbeing of using reactive and proactive strategies.

Learning outcomes

This chapter will help you to:

- explain the difference between the terms proactive and reactive strategies;

- explain the importance of maintaining a person centred approach when establishing proactive strategies;

- identify the proactive and reactive strategies that could be used in your role;

- explain the importance of identifying patterns of behaviour and triggers to challenging behaviour;

- explain the importance of reinforcing positive behaviour with a person you support;

- understand the impact on a person's wellbeing of using reactive and proactive strategies.

Defining proactive and reactive strategies

The famous management author Stephen Covey said in *The 7 Habits of Highly Effective People* (2004), 'Reactive people focus on circumstances over which they have no control. The negative energy generated by that focus, combined with neglect in areas they could do something about, causes their circle of influence to shrink. Proactive people focus their efforts on the things they can do something about. The nature of their energy is positive, enlarging, and magnifying, causing their circle of influence to increase.'

Thinking point

Are you a proactive person? That is, someone who takes the initiative and comes up with new ideas and ways of getting things done. Or are you a reactive person who reacts to a situation rather than taking the initiative?

When we think about supporting people whose behaviour is seen as challenging, the concept of working in a proactive or reactive way is important, as it will inform how you and others respond to the person and their behaviour. How you respond can have a significant impact on the person and their wellbeing.

Proactive strategies or primary prevention strategies: These are the strategies you implement when you have a detailed understanding of a person and can often anticipate the behaviours they are likely to demonstrate.

Proactive or primary prevention strategies are put in place to prevent the person's behaviours presenting a risk to themselves or other people. The first step in any proactive or primary prevention strategy is to observe the person and their behaviour(s) and try to prevent or reduce the risk associated with the behaviours. Proactive strategies involve changing aspects of the person's environment to reduce the likelihood that challenging behaviour will occur.

Reactive or emergency strategies: These are strategies used in response to situations of risk. Reactive strategies are used to manage an immediate risk;

reactive strategies do not aim to achieve long term behaviour change with the person.

Reactive strategies tend to be used with the primary aim of taking control of a difficult situation and minimising any immediate negative outcome or risk.

There should be an individualised primary prevention strategy for each person who presents a challenge. This sets out how the person should be supported to meet their needs as well as giving details of how to respond to particular incidents of challenging, violent or aggressive behaviour.

Some care or support plans also have a secondary prevention strategy or plan. This sets out for the people supporting the person the actions to take once a combination of personal and environmental factors and/or a trigger have created a sequence of behaviours that could escalate into violence or aggression. The aim of secondary prevention is to stop the behaviour building up into a full blown incident. A specific secondary prevention strategy will vary from person to person.

Maintaining a person centred approach when establishing proactive strategies

A key priority in your role supporting a person with a learning disability or a person with autism whose behaviour is seen as challenging is preventing incidents of challenging behaviour, violence and aggression and minimising any need to use restrictive physical interventions. Central to this is having strong person centred values in the organisation that you work for, which then permeate through to the person's day to day support. Person centred values are the foundation of good day to day support for all people with a learning disability and people with autism. They include:

- upholding people's human rights;
- supporting choice;
- promoting independence;
- respecting privacy;
- treating people with dignity;
- working in partnership;
- promoting equality and inclusion;

- respecting individuality;
- promoting friendships and relationships.

You can find out more about person centred values in the book by Liz Tilly in this series: *Person Centred Approaches when Supporting People with a Learning Disability* (2011).

Activity

Choose four of the person centred values shown in the diagram above. For each value that you have identified, think about two ways in which you have demonstrated the value in supporting a person who is considered to challenge your service. Discuss your ideas with your colleagues at your next team meeting.

When working in a person centred way the first step is to assess the behaviour or behaviours which cause concern or present a risk to the person or others. The checklist below will help you to consider the stages in developing a proactive and person centred strategy. You can find out more in the book by John Harris et al. (2008), *Physical Interventions. A Policy Framework*.

Checklist for developing a person centred proactive strategy

1. Do you fully understand the behaviour which is causing concern and why people are concerned about it? You should consider if the behaviour is one which presents a real risk. Do you understand the factors that increase the likelihood of the behaviour occurring?

2. How often is the behaviour exhibited and what situations are likely to increase the frequency with which the behaviour will be expressed?

3. Who is present when the behaviour or behaviours occur? Are there times when crowds increase the likelihood of the behaviour? Might certain people be more likely to be present when a particular behaviour is used?

4. What is the impact of the behaviour on the person and others who come into contact with them? Is the consequence of the behaviour one which requires a response? Is it possible that the behaviour is an 'allowable eccentricity' in that there is no perceivable risk? Is the behaviour just socially odd?
   For example, Josh chooses not to use chairs of any type, preferring to sit on the floor, stand or lean against the edge of tables. When Josh visits the local pub he will sit on the floor next to the table where his friends are sitting. If Josh orders a meal he will put it onto a chair, remain seated on the floor and eat his meal off the chair.

This is an example of a 'socially unusual' behaviour. The impact on Josh is very low, Josh has no problem with his behaviour and it may be that the behaviour in itself decreases his level of anxiety in social situations. There is no obvious risk with the behaviour on a day to day basis either to Josh or to others. Arguably, this behaviour does not require a response over and above day to day monitoring to ensure Josh doesn't sit somewhere where the risk increases to him or other people.

If you work in person centred ways, this will increase the opportunities you have to recognise any changes in behaviour. This is because your understanding of the person helps you to recognise when their behaviour is changing.

Here are some important points to bear in mind:

- Make sure that you continually assess the person, including how they are behaving with any changes in their behaviour identified. Even small changes in how a person is behaving can be important.

- Ensure that there is good communication between the people in the team who are supporting the person. This will include all of the professionals and support workers as well as family and friends.

Proactive strategies include opportunities for the person to engage in positive activities.

- Ensure that agreed approaches are applied with consistency. This may require people to share information across services and service settings.

- Make sure that you review information that is available on a regular basis.

- Ensure that any short term goals continue to be motivating for the person you are supporting and that achievements, positive responses and interactions are recognised and acknowledged.

- Increase the opportunities for the person to engage in positive activities that increase their social skills, including taking part in their local community.

- Support the person to express their individuality, including their cultural and spiritual identity.

- Support the person to develop a range of relationships.

Person centred approaches when establishing strategies means:

assessing the person, noting changes in behaviour, being aware of factors which may affect them

reviewing, reporting and recording, and ensuring there is good communication between team members

increasing motivation by setting achievable goals

being consistent when supporting the person

supporting positive relationships

ensuring the person has a good communication plan and everyone knows how to communicate with them

valuing spiritual and cultural identity and supporting personal expression

Identifying the proactive and reactive strategies that could be used in your role

When you are considering the proactive and reactive strategies you might use in your role, it is important that you take a person centred and partnership approach. The strategies that you adopt and the plans you make must have the person, their family and friends at the centre. All of the strategies and plans need to be developed in partnership with the person, their family carers and any other workers and professionals involved with the person's support.

Positive behaviour support approaches should be developed on an individual basis and built on the observations and understanding of the person concerned. The person's support plan must not concentrate solely on aspects of behaviour, but must cover the overall needs of the person. Their family and friends should be involved, as much as they wish, or is appropriate, in agreeing the support plan.

The person's support plan should address some or all of the following areas:

- Identifying activities they would like to be involved in or new experiences they would like to have. These may need to be introduced slowly and carefully depending on the person's need for routine and predictability.

- Introducing new experiences over time with additional support when necessary.

- Identifying life goals and a pathway to achieve them.

- Ensuring that all of the person's healthcare needs are taken care of and there is access to primary healthcare including their GP, dentist, therapists and access to psychology and counselling.

- Developing routines that meet the person's needs and help them to feel safe and secure.

- Ensuring that the person lives in a safe and secure environment which is designed to meet their needs.

- Supporting functional communication and access to speech and language therapy support if necessary.

Additionally, a positive behaviour support plan should include the following:

- Well recorded achievable goals, which should include long term goals (such as, John would like to be able to shop at the supermarket for half an hour without starting to scream) and short term goals (such as, John will go into the supermarket and buy one item).

- Examples of positive choices that the person can make which may impact on reducing their behaviour.

- Information that identifies why behaviours happen and the factors that are likely to increase the risk of a behaviour occurring.

- Details of how trigger factors that increase the risk of a behaviour being exhibited will be removed or reduced.

- Details of how the person will be supported to increase their skills and how they will be supported to have positive experiences.

- Descriptions of how team members will reinforce the positive behaviours that the person uses and how they will increase opportunities for positive behaviours to be expressed.

- Details for developing a plan to eliminate the behaviours which are of concern or present a risk to the person and others.

- Details of proactive strategies for supporting the person.

Primary prevention is achieved by altering the experiences of the person based on a hypothesis about the causes of the behaviour we would like to prevent. This can be achieved by:

- avoiding significant environmental and personal conditions wherever and whenever possible;

- removing triggers for the behaviour(s) of concern;

- reducing as much as possible whatever causes the person to be stressed;

- ensuring the individual's needs are met;

- creating opportunities to engage in positive activities;

- ensuring the person is involved in their support as much as possible and that those who know them well are included too.

Secondary prevention procedures should be established and agreed, before they are required, to ensure that risky episodes are supported appropriately with proactive strategies. Secondary prevention refers to what you need to do in response to any increasing risk when a particular behaviour is escalating and primary prevention has been tried but has been ineffective. At this point you should be implementing approaches which you expect will calm a situation by diverting attention or de-escalating the person. This can be achieved through the following actions:

- Use calming approaches based on your knowledge of the person, think about what you say and how you say it, and use calm body language.

- Convey confidence but try not to be over assertive as this may be viewed as aggressive.

- Try to divert the person's attention to an activity they enjoy.

- Reduce demands on the person – don't give instructions, but offer the person options.

- Think about any environmental changes which could be made to decrease the state of arousal the person is experiencing.

- Decide who may be the best person to interact with the person when they are stressed or angry; usually this will be someone who knows the person well.

- Look for a win-win option. Your aim is to calm the person and help them manage their emotional state.

When considering the possible proactive strategies that you could use in your role you should consider the following:

- Reducing the factors that increase stress for the person.

- Changing specific environmental conditions, if this is possible.

- Trying to prevent known triggers.

- Reviewing communication strategies and developing positive opportunities for communication.

- Enabling the person to engage in positive activities, creating opportunities for new experiences and skills acquisition.

- Changing how the team interacts with the person. Are there any strategies that could be employed to increase positive interactions? Does the team need to change its approach?

'Reactive strategies' or 'reactive management strategies' which manage behaviours may include environmental change, physical interventions, seclusion, and the use of medication or mechanical restraint. It has been suggested that up to half of people with learning disabilities who also exhibit behaviours viewed as challenging may be exposed to reactive management strategies.

Activity

Think about one person you support. Make a list of all of the proactive and reactive strategies you and the other people supporting the person might use to provide person centred support for them. Discuss your list with a senior colleague and explain your preferred options.

Identifying patterns of behaviour and triggers to challenging behaviour

Patterns of behaviour

Good recording is central to identifying patterns of behaviour and triggers to challenging behaviour. This starts with focused observation and an understanding of how to record behaviour. Below are two examples of behavioural recording:

1. Freda was really angry today and spent the whole day in a mood. Her sister called to say she wouldn't be visiting later today as planned.

2. Freda ate her breakfast and appeared to be happy; she was very chatty and ate all her breakfast. Shortly after breakfast she received a call from her sister who is unwell and unable to visit later today as planned. Freda was upset and cried following this phone call. Freda went to her room and has refused to come out or be persuaded to join in any activities although she was happy to have a couple of drinks during the morning.

The first is an example of poor recording which just tells the reader that Freda has been 'in a mood'. It doesn't help the reader to understand why Freda may be in a mood or what events may have had an impact on Freda's behaviour.

The second example not only tells us how Freda has been behaving but also gives an insight into the events which may have contributed to Freda's mood on the day in question.

Recording must be accurate, up to date, complete and legible and as detailed as possible if it is to be helpful to team members and others. It can then contribute to developing good behaviour support plans and determining which proactive approaches are most likely to have an impact in achieving long term behaviour change. Behavioural recording must be specific to the individual.

Recording checklist
- Make your recording specific to the individual person.
- The record should detail exactly which behaviour(s) are of concern at this point in time.
- It should record when the behaviour occurs and its frequency.
- Recording should detail who is present when the behaviour occurs.
- There should be detailed information on the behaviour or incident being reported which is honest and accurate.
- There should be information on the outcomes or natural consequences of a behaviour or incident.

Making your recording of behaviour detailed and accurate will help inform the behaviour support plans and will:

- enable behaviour interventions to be well targeted;
- improve the quality of support that can be offered and enable individualised strategies to be developed based on the type of behaviour, the reasons it occurs, where it occurs and the frequency of the behaviour;
- reduce the level of risk to the person and those who have contact with them;
- indicate when risk is increasing and enable the team to respond appropriately;
- reduce inappropriate strategies or even abusive practice;
- enable monitoring of the behaviour and the application of proactive approaches;
- monitor the use of restrictive practices if they are being implemented;
- ensure policy and practice are well supported;
- support the development of appropriate staff training when behaviour patterns are reviewed.

You can find out more about record keeping and observation in the book in this series, *Handling Information for Learning Disability Workers* by Lesley Barcham and Jackie Pountney.

Understanding triggers

One of the most simple proactive approaches we can apply in practice is to identify the factors which increase the likelihood of any behaviour occurring. The term often used to describe such factors is the 'setting conditions' for the behaviour. Setting conditions can be split into two simple categories, environmental factors and personal factors. You can find out more about personal and environmental factors in Chapter 1.

Thinking point

Think about your own experiences and what affects how you feel. What things affect your mood in a positive and negative way? What is most likely to affect how you behave towards other people? Try and list these under personal and environmental factors.

If we can remove the environmental factors or setting conditions it may be possible to reduce the frequency of some behaviours. One problem is that human behaviour is very complex and it is usual that more than one factor contributes to a particular behaviour. In fact there are usually many factors which affect a person's behaviour. It can be the case that setting conditions occur with a trigger event, something which increases anxiety within the person, which then leads to a behaviour. A trigger is often specific to the person and their particular situation.

John is 27 years old. He has an autistic spectrum condition and a moderate learning disability. He lives with his mother and brother Peter who is 21. Peter is studying at university close to home.

John returned home after his day at work in the local library. John had not had a good day at work; he got behind on some of his work and his supervisor spoke to him about being more organised. This meant he left work late and he was very anxious about missing his usual bus home. In fact, he only just made it in time to the bus stop. John was looking forward to coming home and relaxing and watching his favourite TV programme on his own. But when he got home his brother and two of his student friends were in the living room drinking beer and watching DVDs. John's plans were completely ruined and he also really disliked the smell of beer. All this change made John really distressed. He shouted at his brother and tipped some of the beer over him and his friends. John stormed out of the room and slammed the door just as his mother was coming downstairs. Hearing the noise she asked John whether he had had a good day and John pushed her hard against the wall and shouted at the top of his voice 'I hate you! I hate you!'

Activity

In John's story, what were the environmental factors that contributed to John being so upset?

What were the triggers which caused John to pour beer over his brother and his friends?

How might the situation have been prevented?

When we have identified the possible triggers of behaviour, it may be possible to develop a hypothesis for a behaviour. In other words, we might be able to identify the factors that increase the likelihood of a behaviour occurring and the reasons why the person carries out the behaviour. These may be described as the functions of behaviour.

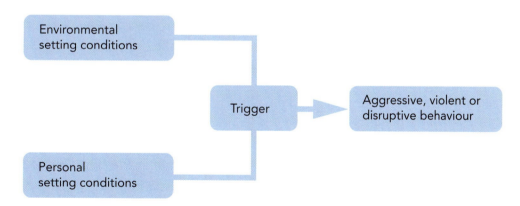

A behaviour may be beneficial or work for a person if it helps them to:

- **gain sensations** – the behaviour can enable the person to feel elated or experience other sensations that they find enjoyable;

- **avoid sensations** – it may be that the environment is too noisy, too hot or too cold and the behaviour enables the person to escape the situation;

- **avoid tasks** – the person may find certain tasks difficult and knows that exhibiting the behaviour will mean that the tasks can be avoided;

- **express their own experience of emotional and cognitive conflict** – this may be a totally irrational belief such as a feeling of failure when trying to learn new skills, and exhibiting behaviour may be a way to express this feeling of frustration;

- **avoid people** – tasks that require co-operation with others may be difficult and this can lead to behaviours that support avoidance;

- **obtain tangibles** – the person knows that the behaviour will gain a tangible 'reward'; it may be something they can use or particularly like, such as the opportunity to read a book or watch a DVD;

- **interact and communicate** – the behaviour may be the primary way the person has of interacting with others, usually because they have not developed other ways of communicating or have difficulty in understanding other people.

Explaining the importance of reinforcing positive behaviour

Activity

If there is a person you support that you struggle to like, try to find a colleague who has more positive feelings towards them. Take as many opportunities as you can to observe your colleague interacting with this person. Look at their facial expressions and behaviour and also the responses from the person that you have not previously observed. Does your colleague genuinely take pleasure in being with the person? Can you see why? Can you start to borrow or share your colleague's feelings towards that person? Discuss what you have learnt from this activity with an experienced colleague.

One way in which you can encourage positive behaviour in the people that you support is to take a positive approach in the way you interact with them and their families.

Often it is difficult to feel very positive, especially if you:

- dislike the person you are supporting or you feel afraid of them at certain times;

- feel frustrated by what appears to be a lack of progress;

- feel anger towards the person because they have injured someone else or you.

All of the above are quite normal and understandable experiences and emotions. It is usual that challenging personal experiences will provoke strong human responses. It is not unusual to experience such emotions or feelings – what is important is how you respond to these feelings and how you manage them when you are working to positively support a person.

Most behaviour will have a positive incentive or a negative consequence. People should be supported to develop a range of socially acceptable behaviours. It may be useful to think about the behaviour of someone you support and what acts as a positive incentive to their behaviour which is viewed as challenging or risky.

Activity

Consider a person you support who sometimes presents behaviours that you find challenging. Make a list of all the activities that he or she likes doing and when they are less likely to present behaviour that challenges. Note down how you know this: was it through observation, asking the person or being told by someone else who knows them well? Does the list of likes provide you with ideas about how you might support the person in learning non challenging behaviours and in identifying areas where you could reinforce positive behaviour?

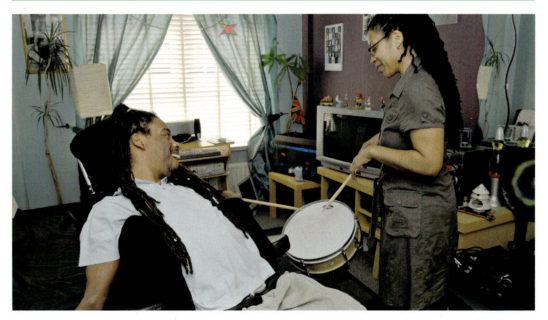

There are many simple ways to positively reinforce a person's non challenging behaviour, including encouraging activities which they enjoy.

Thinking about how you personally communicate and interact with a person can help to support the positive approaches that you can use, including:

- Do you engage in activities with the person or simply act as a bystander while they are taking part? For example, do you go swimming with them or just sit at the side and watch them swim?

- Is your body language open and does it convey that you trust the person? Does it convey that they can trust you?

- Do you listen to what they say? Do you always act on what is said to you or what you say you will do?

- Are you aware of a person's emotional state and do you respond appropriately to it?

- Are you quick to offer positive feedback and comments whenever the opportunity is available? For example, saying thank you when a person helps with a household task: 'Thank you, John, for doing all for the washing up tonight, it was a great help to everyone.'

- Do you support the person when they are learning new skills? Sometimes a person will take a long time to learn something new. They may lack confidence and exhibiting behaviour could be a way of avoiding stressful situations or showing and expressing their fears.

- Do you have fun? Sharing jokes, listening to personal stories and sharing activities all help in building trusting relationships. When we are having fun we can create opportunities for learning new skills and engaging in new opportunities. Although you must consider appropriate professional boundaries, this should not be a barrier to providing positive support.

Evaluating the impact of using reactive rather than proactive strategies

It is important that any use of a reactive strategy is usually only considered as a last resort. This is when no other alternative proactive strategies would reduce the risk and lead to the same outcome. It is commonly agreed that reactive management strategies fulfil two primary functions:

1. Reducing the immediate risk to the person and to others.

2. Providing workers with an option which will 'control' the person and the behaviour at a time of increased risk.

However, reactive management strategies will not support a person to achieve long term behaviour change, nor should they be viewed as part of a positive behaviour support plan. In addition, there are risks associated with the use of reactive management strategies, as discussed earlier in this chapter, which include physical harm and psychological trauma to support staff as well as to the person exposed to possible interventions.

If services implement strategies which include the use of physical interventions, they should ensure that such approaches are individualised. Staff must have access to and attend appropriate training to ensure an understanding that such strategies are at the end of a continuum of approaches which should be implemented to bring about a resolution to the situation.

It is possible that the use of physical interventions may lead to:

- a breakdown in any therapeutic relationship;
- a person feeling that they are being punished;
- a person experiencing severe trauma linked to previous experiences or the event itself;
- a person exhibiting an increase in the frequency of their behaviour;
- physical injury;
- negative consequences for the person who exhibits the behaviour;
- negative consequences for the staff team supporting the person or their family carers;
- disagreement between the staff team on the best way to provide support;
- guilt and feelings of failure on the part of the staff team or family carers.

Other reactive management strategies may include the following:

- An over reliance on confrontation, such as shouting at the person or using aggressive body language or tone of voice. Responding with the same level of emotional arousal and behaviour exhibited by a person is not helpful. It is likely to increase arousal and lead to a more serious consequence as a result.
- Punishment which may be viewed as abusive practice. Threatening to stop a person doing an activity they enjoy or implying that you might hurt them or abuse them in any other way is not acceptable. In behavioural terms you must not implement consequences to try and reduce the frequency of behaviour or to punish a person.

In contrast, proactive strategies that are based on person centred values and approaches will enhance your relationship with the person and build positive experiences for them.

Key points from this chapter

- It is important to assess behaviour comprehensively and to understand the function and causes of the behaviour for each individual.

- Proactive strategies should be employed to prevent behaviours escalating and to reduce risk.

- There are environmental and personal factors which will affect the individual and may increase the risk of behaviours being exhibited.

- Using a proactive approaches checklist will ensure you have considered factors which could be important in reducing risks associated with behaviours.

- Plans must be individualised and based on detailed and accurate behaviour assessment.

- Ensuring plans are appropriate for supporting an individual's assessed needs will increase the likelihood of positive outcomes for people.

References and where to go for more information

References

Allen, D (ed.) (2002) *Ethical Approaches to Physical Interventions. Volume I: Responding to challenging behaviour in people with intellectual disabilities.* Kidderminster: BILD

Allen, D (ed.) (2009) *Ethical Approaches to Physical Interventions. Volume II: Changing the agenda.* Kidderminster: BILD

Barcham, L and Pountney, J (2011) *Handling Information for Learning Disability Workers.* Exeter: Learning Matters/BILD

BILD (2010) *BILD Code of Practice for the Use and Reduction of Physical Interventions*, third edition. Kidderminster: BILD

Covey, S (2004) *The 7 Habits of Highly Effective People.* New York: Free Press

Harris, J et al. (2008) *Physical Interventions. A Policy Framework. Second edition.* Kidderminster: BILD

Tilly, L (2011) *Person Centred Approaches when Supporting People with a Learning Disability.* Exeter: Learning Matters/BILD

Chapter 3

Responding to incidents of challenging behaviour

As a young nurse I remember talking to an older person I supported who had spent much of her life in institutions. Alice (not her real name) was then in her late sixties and living in a small community home. Most of the time she refused to leave the building, occasionally venturing into the garden to watch the birds and enjoy a cup of tea. Alice had entered an old asylum as a young lady where she was described as 'delinquent'. Later she was moved to a secure hospital and had only recently moved to the residential home she lived in. The lady I knew was far from 'delinquent', she was funny, quite articulate when she had her teeth in and had a love of police officers, especially when they were in uniform.

The behaviour that had led to Alice being in so much trouble when she was in the asylum was starting a fire; this had resulted in her being sent to a secure hospital for many years. When I was talking to her about her past and chatting about her experiences, I asked why she had started the fire. With a laugh, Alice replied, 'Because I hated where I was living and no one would listen. I knew that they would have to move me after that. Then they would listen.'

Sharon Paley talking about her early professional experiences

Christopher was being supported to attend the dentist and all the preparation work had been done. On the journey to the surgery he appeared to be calm and happy, chatting about his breakfast and plan to go bowling that evening. On arrival at the surgery he bounded out of the car running towards the door. Just as his support worker managed to catch up with him he suddenly sat on the floor, shouting, 'I'm not going in, I'm not, hate it, hate it!' Fran, Christopher's support worker, said 'C'mon Chris it'll be fine.' As she said that, Chris hit Fran hard on the leg and began to bite his hand. Fran moved to one side so she was just out of his reach and watched Chris closely. She did not respond verbally but crouched so he could be at eye level with her. Chris started to calm and after a while Fran held her hand out to him. Chris and Fran stood up. 'Do you think we should go in now?' asked Fran. 'We can go for a drink in the park afterwards.' Chris replied, 'I'd like that.' Then slowly he went into the surgery with Fran. Fran managed this incident well. She gave Chris space, allowed him time to think about his options and didn't give him too much verbal information. In his own time Chris decided he could go into the dentists' surgery and his check up went well.

Introduction

How we respond to other people will have an impact on how they respond to us. It's a simple fact of life – my reaction causes your reaction and how I behave affects how you behave. It is important to bear this in mind when considering how you can respond to incidents of challenging behaviour. In this chapter you will learn about the five stages of arousal used in most incident management, and how to respond at each stage. We will also look at techniques for defusing challenging incidents, which emphasise the need to stay calm during confrontations. This chapter also considers the importance of maintaining the dignity and respect of everyone involved in an incident. In addition, you will learn about the need to complete records accurately and objectively following an incident of challenging behaviour in line with agreed ways of working.

In this chapter you will explore different types of behaviours which might be described as 'challenging' and why. You will be asked to reflect on how your experiences affect your view of different behaviours and the impact those behaviours have upon you.

Learning outcomes

This chapter will help you to:

- identify types of challenging behaviours;
- demonstrate how to respond to incidents of challenging behaviour by following behaviour support plans and agreed ways of working;
- explain the steps that are taken to maintain the dignity of and respect for an individual when responding to incidents of challenging behaviour;
- explain and demonstrate how to complete records accurately and objectively in line with work setting requirements following an incident of challenging behaviour.

Types of challenging behaviours

People who have a learning disability and people with autism may be described as having challenging behaviour if their behaviour has an impact on their life; that is, if their behaviour:

- increases the risk of harm to them or others;

- restricts their access to social and educational opportunities and restricts their lifestyle, either in the short or long term;

- affects their general health and wellbeing;

- is socially or culturally unacceptable;

- increases the risk of them committing a criminal offence;

- gives rise to plans or actions by others that may restrict their liberty;

- increases the risk of exposure to restrictive practices such as physical restraint or seclusion.

It may be that only a few of the points listed above relate to a person whom you consider as having behaviour described as challenging.

Before we can discuss the different types of challenging behaviour, it is helpful to think about how people view behaviours and then apply the label of 'challenging behaviour' to them. We all have our personal views of behaviours, and this means that what we believe to be challenging will vary from what our colleagues believe.

For example, Lennon has worked in services for people with a learning disability for over six years. He has worked for three years in a service that supports people who exhibit behaviours which are described as challenging. When he was asked which five behaviours he found to be the most challenging to work with, he ranked them as follows (with 1 being the most challenging):

1. Self injurious behaviour.

2. Aggression towards colleagues and others.

3. Withdrawal from activities.

4. Aggression towards him.

5. Swearing.

Sheila has worked in services for people with autism for 14 years across a range of services for children and adults. Sheila has also worked in services for people who exhibit behaviours described as challenging. She listed the most 'challenging' behaviours as:

1. Being ignored.

2. A person withdrawing and not responding to requests.

3. Bullying and racism.

4. Verbal challenges and arguments.

5. Physical aggression.

The two examples show how two different people providing support can have very different opinions about what is challenging, depending on their experience. A person's view of behaviour may also be affected by their values and beliefs. Lennon dislikes swearing because he believes it to be wrong and he doesn't swear himself. This in turn affects his attitude to how challenging he perceives swearing to be because he finds it offensive on a personal level.

Thinking point

Think about your own experience of behaviours that you believe to be challenging and answer the following questions:

1. *Why do you believe the behaviours to be challenging?*

2. *How do your values and beliefs affect your response to any behaviour?*

3. *Do you think other people share your views?*

Behaviour may be described as challenging because:

- it has negative consequences for the person themselves;
- there are negative consequences for those who live with, support, or care for the person;
- it increases the risk of harm to the person;
- it increases the risk to other people who are in contact with the person;
- there is an impact on the person's lifestyle and opportunities;
- the person and others around them are likely to be more socially isolated as a consequence of the behaviour;

- the behaviour can lead to exclusion from services or activities;
- it can have an impact on the person's health and on their ability to access healthcare.

Behaviours which are generally described as challenging

1. **Physical violence** – this is usually directed towards others, who may or may not be known to the person. This may include, for example, hitting other people or throwing things at others to hurt them.

2. **Self-injury** – these are acts of violence against oneself which cause injury. Examples of self injury include hitting oneself, banging limbs on objects or skin picking.

3. **Verbal Aggression** – this includes shouting and swearing at others, making abusive remarks or verbal threats to others.

4. **Bullying, harassment or racism** – these are directly offensive or threatening behaviours often directed at a person to cause them personal distress. This could include verbal or racial abuse.

5. **Impulsive behaviours** – these can include risk taking behaviours such as running into roads, stealing or inappropriate sexual behaviour.

6. **Damaging the environment** – such behaviour can include damaging personal property, furniture or surroundings.

7. **Passive behaviour** – this can include refusing to cooperate or comply with requests or withdrawal from social situations.

8. **Criminal behaviours** – these are behaviours which are illegal and could result in the person being charged with criminal offences such as arson, physical assaults on other people or stealing.

This list is not exhaustive and it is likely you can think of other behaviours which may be described as challenging.

Responding to an incident of challenging behaviour

Let's consider practical suggestions for skilful incident management by looking at how this should work with acts of violent or aggressive behaviour. This can include the build up of anger or other forms of acting out behaviour. The principles and techniques considered here in reaction to a violent or aggressive incident illustrate how to avoid conflict and confrontation in relation to other types of challenging behaviour. Appropriate responses from staff to this sort of situation contribute to good practice.

Good incident management requires people or supporters to follow individualised proactive strategies and to develop good team approaches, which then ensure consistent responses to the person. Best practice is having a detailed agreed behaviour support plan that sets out how to respond to a person during an incident of challenging behaviour. This should outline the different stages and responses to situations of emotional arousal, which may be expressed with aggressive or violent behaviour or responses such as running away from a situation.

Every person that you support who presents behaviour that challenges should have a behaviour support plan that sets out:

- the proactive preventative strategies that staff should be following to reduce the challenging behaviour occurring;
- details about what to do and how to support the person during an incident of challenging behaviour.

You should use this support plan together with the relevant policies and procedures relating to positive behaviour support when considering good incident management.

Activity

Take some time to look at the policies and procedures of your organisation. List all of those that might be relevant to your work when you are supporting someone and that focus on promoting positive behaviour and incident management. Check with your line manager or a senior colleague as to whether you have identified all of the relevant policies. If you work as a personal assistant and are employed directly by the person you support, they may not have all of the policies and procedures you might expect if you worked for a social care provider. Instead, your employer should have set out the expected and agreed ways of working and provided them for you in your contract of employment or in separate policy documents. They should tell you what you should do in particular situations, including if you suspect abuse, if there has been a breach of confidentiality or how to respond to an incident of challenging behaviour. Once you have listed the relevant policies or agreed ways of working, take some time to read them and note down how they influence what you do in relation to positive behaviour support and managing an incident.

Activity

Now look at both the support or care plan and the behaviour support plan of a person you work with who is known to present behaviour that sometimes challenges your service. In addition, look at any recent incident reports that have been completed. Which policies and procedures or agreed ways of working underpin the support being provided?

General information on managing an incident

There are five stages that people typically pass though before, during and after an outburst of aggressive or violent behaviour. Other behaviours such as temper tantrums or screaming fits may also follow this pattern.

The five stages of arousal:

1. Trigger

2. Build up

3. Crisis

4. Recovery

5. Post incident depression

We will now examine the five stages, describing the typical behaviour and what actions to take, when and how. The stages are shown in the graph below. This provides a useful way of remembering the sequence of events that occurs during most incidents.

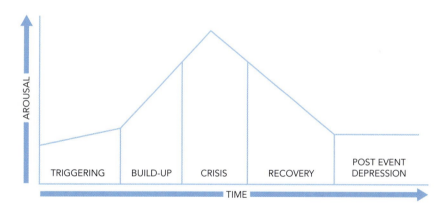

The five stages of a violent incident.

What is meant by arousal?

Arousal describes the ways in which our minds and bodies respond to what is happening around us, such as when we are emotionally upset, feeling anxious, confused, distressed or angry. With any of these feelings, the chemical activity in the body and brain changes and this affects what you do and the way you do it. You know these changes are taking place when:

- your heart starts beating faster;
- your rate of breathing goes up;
- you feel your muscles tightening;
- you get warm flushed feelings;
- you get butterflies in your stomach.

The graph below shows arousal as a dotted line. The higher the line goes up, the greater the arousal. Normal arousal is shown by the straight dotted line and this is what you are like when you are watching TV, resting, chatting quietly with someone or simply feeling peaceful and happy. As a person becomes more aroused the dotted line starts to move upwards as shown in the second graph below. This reflects what happens when a person becomes upset or angry.

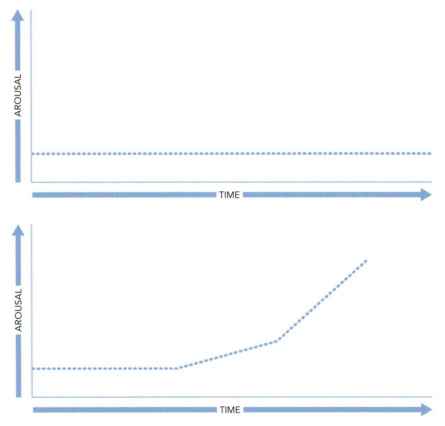

Normal arousal and heightened arousal.

Each of the five stages may vary in length. Some people go from the trigger phase through build up to crisis in a matter of seconds. Others may have a 'slow burn' and may take days to reach crisis. While most people respond in one way or the other, there are always complex individuals whose pattern of arousal sometimes occurs quickly and at other times very slowly.

The five stages of arousal

1. **Trigger: the person is exposed to a trigger event which leads to emotional arousal**

   Triggers are highly personal. A trigger for one person is not a trigger for another. Triggers are often things that happen around the person, but they can also be things that happen inside the person such as illness, pain, discomfort or distressing thoughts.

   Examples of triggers may include:

   - being hungry;
   - being startled or scared;
   - feeling distressed;
   - being in a noisy environment;
   - a special activity being cancelled;
   - a predictable routine being disrupted;
   - being told no;
   - being shouted at;
   - being hit;
   - being near someone who is angry.

2. **Build up: the person experiences a rise in their emotional state**

   During build up people may show outward behaviours which indicate that their emotional state is changing, for example you may see someone start to behave in unpredictable ways, including breathing heavily or becoming verbally abusive to the people around them. Sometimes the changes appear slowly and are quite subtle while sometimes they are more dramatic and occur suddenly. Typical build up changes include:

   - increased activity;
   - fidgeting;
   - an inability to sit still;
   - breathing quickly;
   - talking rapidly;
   - abusive or aggressive language;
   - sweating and flushing;
   - not agreeing to simple requests.

3. **Crisis: the person is in a state of high emotional arousal and may exhibit high risk behaviour**

   Crisis usually only lasts for a brief period of time and is most often expressed in behaviours we would associate with high emotional states. The person may behave in ways that include:

   - being verbally aggressive towards others;
   - showing physical aggression towards others;
   - destroying property;
   - hurting or injuring themselves.

   Normally, people do not stay in crisis for long. Sometimes it can feel like a long time but this is when the person is staying very aroused and near crisis for an extended period. If there are triggers that remain, or if the way people respond to them has become a trigger, then the person can have a series of crises one after another.

4. **Recovery: the person enters a phase of reduced emotional arousal and starts to calm**

   After crisis, there is a period of recovery where the person will gradually calm. If there are no further triggers the person will gradually calm down and return to normal arousal. This period should be managed with care as people can be 're-triggered' and enter crisis again.

5. **Post event depression: the person feels low after the crisis**

   A post event depression follows the recovery phase and is a period when the person may 'dip' below their own usual emotional state. They may feel very lethargic, experience low mood or even feel quite depressed. In response to this the person may withdraw from social contact or refuse to engage in conversation or activities. Not everyone seems to experience this stage; some people get back to their normal state of arousal without any visible effects as if nothing has happened.

Some people may go through the stages very quickly; others may take much longer, even taking hours or days to experience each arousal state.

Activity

Go back to the support plan, behaviour support plan and incident reports that you used for the previous activity. Does the person they refer to usually go through the five stages as set out above, or not? Identify any differences and discuss them with your line manager or someone else who knows the person well. Make sure you know how the person typically behaves during each of the five stages.

Actions and proactive approaches to managing an incident

Practical steps you can take that will help you when managing an incident or preparing before you need to manage an incident include the following:

- Get to know the person well so that you know how they behave on a day to day basis and when they are in a good mood state. It's only when you know a person well that you will know if they are behaving 'out of character' and then you can respond appropriately.

- Make sure all of the team who supports the person knows all of the relevant information to enable them to offer good support.

- Ensure that you know the signs that the person's mood state may be changing.

- Ensure that you know the behaviours that are most likely to be exhibited when the person is in a heightened state of arousal.

- Make sure you know what may act as triggers to the person's state of arousal and may change their mood state.

- Make sure you know what might make them feel better.

- Ask the person if they can tell you what may work best for them when they feel upset. Some people feel afraid and want company while other people prefer to be on their own.

General actions to take during the five stages of arousal

1. **Actions to take during triggers**

   The most effective way to reduce potential emotional conflict for the person is to remove the triggers, if they are known to you. In some instances this may not be possible. For example, if the person's trigger is a biological one, perhaps linked to a physical issue, such as toothache or period pains, it may not be possible to remove the trigger. Consider:

   - What are the known triggers?
   - Is it practical to remove the triggers all of the time?
   - Is ongoing assessment continuing to ensure that new triggers are identified and addressed?
   - Are there opportunities for the person to have positive experiences and avoid potential triggers?
   - Is removing the triggers to the person's behaviour in their best interest and will this help them to gain control over their emotional state and the behaviour they exhibit?

2. **Supporting the person during build up**

It is critical that you can recognise when a person's emotional state is building towards crisis. It is during this build up period that you can de-escalate or defuse the situation. This is usually achieved by distracting the person so that they are better able to manage their emotional state and feel calm, rather than progress into crisis. It may be possible to defuse the situation by:

- moving the person from the things in their environment that might have triggered their arousal;
- distracting the person by offering them the calming strategies that have been identified to work for them (this could include a drink, some calming music, a quiet space where they can relax, or spending time in the garden);
- responding to the person calmly and appropriately using language they understand, and responding to any reasonable requests or needs;
- avoiding confrontational responses or approaches;
- reassuring the person and showing that you are calm (even if you do not feel very calm!).

3. **Supporting the person who is in crisis**

When supporting a person who is in a highly aroused state and experiencing crisis it is important to:

- communicate clearly with colleagues;
- ensure you and your colleagues are not at risk;
- ensure you maintain a safe environment for other people who may be at risk;
- keep the person who is exhibiting the behaviour of concern safe and protect them from harm as much as possible, without putting yourself or others at risk;
- try to prevent other people from joining the situation or watching as this can inflame people when they are upset and may increase the intensity of their behaviour;
- keep verbal communication to a minimum;
- keep your body language neutral and predictable.

4. **Supporting the person through recovery**

People can be very vulnerable as they come out of crisis and may experience quite strong emotions and physical sensations. For these reasons, people may be re-triggered and re-enter a crisis state very quickly or without any apparent warning. This will delay the incident being concluded. Once you are sure a person is entering a recovery phase you can:

- observe them;

- ensure that they feel supported by being available, but don't talk at them;

- offer quiet reassurance, which could be low level verbal reassurance or soft touch, such as a calming hand on the person's shoulder or holding their hand if this is appropriate; use your knowledge of the person to offer calming activities that they enjoy, for example a walk with the dog, watching a favourite TV programme or time for them to follow a special interest, such as reading timetables, handling their strings, etc.

5. **Offering support during post event depression**

   Although not everyone will enter a phase of post event depression, for those people who do it is an important time. It allows them to return to their usual demeanour and to make sense of the situation they experienced. It is important to remember that a person can also experience a trigger at this stage in their recovery and re-enter crisis once again. You will know the person well and should use approaches based on your knowledge of the person, which may include:

   - offering quiet reassurance;

   - just 'being' with the person, and using opportunities to discuss the incident as they arise;

   - offering calming distracters which are specific to the person.

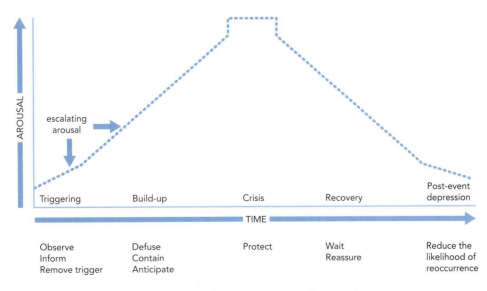

Incident management – action in relation to stages of arousal.

It is important to consider that people do not always behave in predictable ways. For example, not every incident will follow this five stage process. It is also possible that even when you have thoroughly assessed a person and feel you have a good understanding of how they are most likely to behave, they can change their behaviour and therefore their emotional response.

Some behaviours that are described as challenging are not associated with the person experiencing crisis. This includes behaviours that are:

- aimed at gaining increased interaction and communication;

- used to gain particular things, such as food, sweets or DVDs;

- seeking to bring a sense of predictability to the person's situation if it is too stressful for them;

- used to experience some sensations or feelings.

Activity

Consider the support plan, behaviour support plan and incident reports that you have used for the two previous activities. Note down the actions that you and others should take when supporting the person during an incident. Discuss your notes with your line manager or someone else who knows the person well. Are you confident that you know what to do during each stage of an incident to support the person well?

Maintaining dignity and respect when supporting people

In the section in Chapter 2, *Maintaining a person centred approach when establishing proactive strategies*, there is information about the person centred values that need to underpin all your work with people with a learning disability and people with autism. Having strong person centred values based on upholding people's human rights, respecting privacy, and promoting equality and inclusion, are essential to providing good everyday support. This must also underpin support offered in a crisis and whilst managing an incident.

Your judgement as to whether you believe a behaviour is challenging or not is based on your own experience of behaviour and the beliefs you hold about that behaviour. You may believe a particular behaviour is anti-social, unacceptable or offensive and this will have an impact on your response to that behaviour. If you hold negative feelings about a person this will increase your negative opinions of them which are not based in fact. You must work to develop a positive attitude towards the person you support by taking the following actions:

- Acknowledge to yourself (and if you feel confident to do so, to a colleague) any negative feelings toward the person concerned. It is better to admit your feelings and then gradually try to address them and focus on developing positive feelings.

- Reflect on the personal values and attitudes that might be influencing how you react to that person and how they might be limiting your potential to offer better support.

- Take the opportunity to learn from colleagues or others who have more positive feelings towards the person.

Promoting dignity and respect through non confrontational communication

When we find ourselves in stressful situations it is often easy to respond in a negative confrontational way. If we are responding like this to a person who is upset or angry we could make them feel much worse. Confrontational approaches are often perceived as negative by others or can even be viewed as threatening or bullying. Confrontational approaches indicate a lack of respect for the person you are supporting.

Non confrontational styles of communicating and working rely on the ability to offer supportive approaches based on our personal understanding of individuals. It is important to appreciate that positive relationships are based on a shared power base; the essential building block of creating a non confrontational relationship is a shared understanding. You can develop and promote a non confrontational approach and communication style by first considering how the person is likely to communicate with you:

- How does the person choose to communicate?

- Do other people understand what the person is communicating or can just a few key people understand them?

- Does the person understand information they are given or do they need extra help?

- If they use sign language, have all the support team got a good understanding of the signs and do they use them consistently?

- What can be done to increase the opportunities for communication?

Other things you can do to promote a non confrontational way of working include the following:

- Keep your behaviour predictable and simple, don't alarm the person or seek to establish dominance.

- Show that you are listening when they speak by giving them your full attention.

- Do not raise your voice or shout. Keep your tone of voice even, positive and reassuring.

- Use non threatening body postures with your shoulders down and relaxed. Don't put your hands or on your hips, fold your arms, invade the person's personal space or use any other confrontational body language.

In terms of your verbal communication it is important to develop a repertoire of suitable non confrontational responses that can be helpful in defusing a situation.

Confrontational phrases	Non confrontational phrases
'Get back in here'	'Let's go back together'
'Don't do that'	'Let's try it this way'
'Sit down now!'	'How about we sit down and read?'

Sue Thurman's book, *Communicating Effectively with People with a Learning Disability* (2011), and the book by Sue Hatton and Tom Boughton, *An Introduction to Supporting People with Autistic Spectrum Conditions* (2011), both in this series, provide a lot more information on the development of good communication skills.

Checklist for treating people with dignity and respect

Other actions you can take to promote dignity and respect include:

1. Have a zero tolerance of all forms of abuse.

2. Support people with the same respect you would want for yourself or a member of your family.

3. Treat each person as an individual with person centred approaches and support.

4. Enable people to maintain the maximum level of independence, choice and control.

5. Listen and support people to express their needs and wants.

6. Respect people's right to privacy.

7. Ensure people feel able to complain without fear of retribution.

8. Engage with family members as equal care partners.

9. Assist people to maintain confidence and positive self esteem.

10. Act to alleviate people's loneliness and isolation.

Based on the Dignity Challenge. For more information go to:
www.dignityincare.org.uk

Treat each person as an individual with person centred approaches and support.

Activity

Thinking again about the person you have used for the other activities in this chapter, consider how you and others would maintain dignity and respect for that person during an incident of challenging behaviour. For each of the five stages write down two ways that you can maintain their dignity and ensure that they are treated with respect. Discuss this with your line manager or someone who knows the person well.

Completing records accurately and objectively following an incident of challenging behaviour

When you started work supporting people with a learning disability or people with autism you may have been surprised about the amount of record keeping that your job involved. However, records and reports are essential to providing good consistent support. Here is a list of the written records one organisation keeps:

- initial assessments and history;
- day book or handover book;
- medical reports and medication records;
- accident records;
- personal finance records, including bank account details;
- comment and complaints records;
- individual care/support plans;
- person centred plans;
- review report;
- behaviour management plans;
- incident reports;
- adult protection reporting forms;
- risk assessments.

This organisation also keeps other records, such as for fire drills, fridge and freezer temperatures, staff rotas, staff reviews and appraisals. Some of these relate to staff, some to safety and the protection of both staff and individuals and some ensure proper financial management. All are important in a high quality service.

When supporting a person whose behaviour is seen to challenge a service, or when supporting a person as a personal assistant in relation to their behaviour, a number of records are of particular importance to ensure consistent proactive support. These include:

- the person's person centred plan;
- a care or support plan;
- a behaviour support plan;
- incident reports;
- risk assessments.

When you are contributing to these reports, you need to demonstrate that you are working within the legislation and codes of practice that relate to handling information.

The Human Rights Act

The Data Protection Act

Laws, reports and codes of practice to take account of when handling information

The Caldicott Report

The Code of Practice for Social Care Workers

You can find out more about the relevant legislation and how to demonstrate that you are working in line with it in the book in this series by Lesley Barcham and Jackie Pountney, *Handling Information for Learning Disability Workers* (2011).

The records and reports that you contribute to should be up to date, accurate, complete and legible. They should be written and stored safely in line with the policies and procedures of your organisation.

You must maintain clear and accurate records as required by procedures established for your work.

Read the policies and procedures of your organisation that relate to record keeping, confidentiality and data protection. Then look at three recent reports or records that you and your colleagues have contributed to. Check whether they are in line with the policies or procedures. In your view, are the records accurate, legible, complete and objective? This means they are written to a consistent standard, free from error and easily understood. They should also be objective, their factual content being free from any biased statements or opinions.

Activity

Good reporting and recording must be accurate, objective and easily understood. Look at these three examples of recording. Which is the most accurate and objective account of this incident? What makes it accurate and objective? Which account is likely to be the most reliable account of what occurred?

1. *Brian ran into the room aggressively shouting and swearing. He had been in a foul mood all day and we had expected he'd fly off the handle at some point in the day. He was so enraged, he fell over as he went to hit Christina who was watching telly and eating a cake at the time. The cake went everywhere and Christina retaliated, cutting Brian's head with the plate by accident.*

2. *Brian appeared to be upset when he got up today. He refused his breakfast and told Joan he wasn't hungry and was feeling sick. We checked to see if Brian had a temperature earlier today and physically he seemed to be quite well. Although he said he felt sick he has not been sick at all.*

   Brian's low mood state continued for most of the day and he has been unusually quiet. Joan tried to encourage him to feed the birds which he usually enjoys but he told her to 'get off'. Brian spent a couple of hours sleeping this afternoon.

   When he got up he rushed into the room almost running and shouted towards Christina 'I hate you, you're a nasty lady I hate you.' He then went toward Christina as if he was going to hit her but he lost his footing and fell onto her. Christina was eating her cake. She then hit Brian with her plate and as it broke Brian sustained a small cut to his head.

   Brian was helped up and we managed to get him to sit on an arm chair. He seemed to be quite shocked and started to cry.

3. *Christina has had a very active day today and appeared to be happy for the most part. She went horse riding with her sister and came home at 4.00pm. Christina was eating her cake when Brian fell on her; she hit him with her plate causing him to be cut. Christina didn't seem bothered and continued to eat her cake.*

When you complete an incident report or any other record as part of your work, you can use the following checklist to help you assess the accuracy and objectivity of the record:

- Give objective information – fact not opinion.

- Describe the behaviour as accurately as you can.

- Avoid writing what you 'think' the person is feeling or thinking unless they have told you.

- Use language that is non discriminatory and is free from unnecessary jargon or abbreviations.

- Sign and date the record.

- Complete the record in a legible manner.

- Store the record securely in line with the legislation and the policies and procedures of your organisation.

- Ensure that the person the record is about knows they can see the information which is written about them and which affects their health, welfare and support unless it would not be in their best interests.

Key points from this chapter

- We all identify different types of behaviour as challenging.

- Generally behaviour that is seen as challenging includes: physical violence, self injury, verbal aggression, bullying and harassment, impulsive behaviour, damaging the environment, passive behaviour and criminal acts.

- It is important to follow a person's behaviour support plan when responding to an incident of challenging behaviour.

- Try to avoid situations in which a person regularly presents challenging behaviour.

- Actions to take during the five stages of emotional arousal include:

  - during triggers – observe and inform;

  - during build up – defuse, respond and contain;

  - during crisis – protect;

- during recovery – reassure and wait;

- during post-crisis depression – offer support and advice.

- Techniques for de-escalation of emotional arousal include:

  - avoid confrontation;

  - give reassurance;

  - show you are calm;

  - offer alternative activities;

  - avoid an audience.

- Keeping effective records is key to ensuring people with a learning disability and people with autism get good support.

- You need to follow your organisation's policies and procedures on report writing, safeguarding and the management of behaviour when responding to and reporting on incidents of challenging behaviour.

- It is important to have agreed ways of working that are used consistently by team members.

- It is important to maintain the dignity and respect of the person you support when managing an incident of challenging behaviour.

- Following an incident of challenging behaviour, you need to complete records and reports in line with your organisation's policies and procedures that are accurate, objective, legible and complete.

References and where to go for more information

References

Barcham, L and Pountney, J (2011) *Handling Information for Learning Disability Workers.* Exeter: Learning Matters/BILD

Hatton, S and Boughton, T (2011) *An Introduction to Supporting People with Autistic Spectrum Conditions.* Exeter: Learning Matters/BILD

Thurman, L (2011) *Communicating Effectively with People with a Learning Disability.* Exeter: Learning Matters/BILD

Tilly, L (2011) *Person Centred Approaches when Supporting People with a Learning Disability. Exeter:* Learning Matters/BILD

Legislation, policies and reports

Data Protection Act 1998

The Caldicott Report. London: Department of Health 1997

Human Rights Act 1998

The Code of Practice for Social Care Workers

Websites

BILD www.bild.org.uk

Challenging Behaviour Foundation www.thecbf.org.uk

National Autistic Society www.autism.org.uk

Chapter 4

Supporting people following an incident of challenging behaviour

> It was the worst experience of my career. I didn't know what to do or how to react and, worse still, no one would talk about it afterwards; they all just got on with the day to day stuff. No one mentioned the incident and I was very new so didn't know what to expect. I kept going over and over the incident in my mind for weeks and months afterwards, thinking I should have stopped Billie being hurt so badly.
>
> *Reflections of a professional following an incident of aggressive behaviour they had experienced as a student in a service for people with autism and mental health needs.*

Introduction

Our reaction to any incident of challenging behaviour will be very personal. It will be dependent on our previous experiences, the experience of those around us at the time, how we interact with each other and the consequences of the situation as we perceive them.

It's important to consider how all of the people involved in an incident are supported as this can have a profound effect on them over time. They can be traumatised by a challenging incident, particularly if it is of a violent or aggressive nature. This applies to professionals as well as the other people you support, the person's family, friends and other witnesses.

Policies are important in service settings as they set out for workers what they need to do in certain situations. However, in terms of practical application it is often our actions which will ultimately affect the outcome of any situation and the long term wellbeing of all those involved. This chapter will help you to consider how you can best support people after they have been involved in an incident which can be described as challenging.

How to support a person to return to a calm state after exhibiting a challenging behaviour

We all express our feelings in different ways. Following an incident in which someone has exhibited a behaviour that concerns us, the people involved will experience a wide range of emotions and will express them in different ways. The person at the centre of the incident and all who were present may feel:

- sadness;

- anger;

- hurt;

- fear;

- isolation;

- guilt;

- confusion.

It is important that we recognise that any event which has been 'out of the ordinary' may affect people in a variety of ways. Due to the range of emotions that people might feel it is very important to only try to calm a person once they are no longer experiencing 'crisis' (see the diagram below).

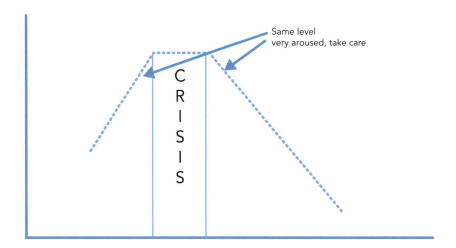

Once a person has passed through crisis and is beginning to return to a calm state you should:

- ensure the person is safe;

- avoid doing anything which may 're-trigger' the behaviour;

- appear calm and relaxed – take a non-confrontational approach but stay close to the person so you can observe them;

- offer reassurance to the person;

- avoid situations where other people gather and watch what is happening;

- offer alternatives which you know the person finds calming, for example play music or offer them a drink.

The actions you should take are best summarised in the ARCH diagram below.

A – avoid – confrontation and situations which might re-trigger the person

R – reassure – the person and others who are in the vicinity. Take the 'heat' out of the situation

C – calm – offer a calming presence in your actions and communications with everyone

H – heal – avoid making a scene and creating an audience, offer alternatives as the person calms and incentives to be calm

Thinking point

Think about a recent incident when you supported someone to return to a calm state. Using the principles of ARCH above, how could you have applied them to the incident and would you have done anything differently?

One useful way to help a person to manage their emotions following an incident is to use a traffic light system, which can be adapted to suit their communication needs. For such an intervention to be helpful everyone involved in supporting the person will need to be consistent in how they use the system and in their responses. In this approach a person has cards which they can show people. The cards help the person to recognise how they are feeling and in turn this may support them to understand their emotions better. It can be helpful if the cards have 'instructions' for staff to follow so the person learns that if they communicate how they are feeling, then staff will respond to them positively and consistently. For example:

I'm feeling OK and will be happy to take part in activities or join a group.

I am not feeling too good and would like to spend some time in the relaxation room listening to music.

I am not feeling good and might get cross. Please offer me a drink, a DVD or opportunity to go into the garden. I may need help and may not speak to you.

Supporting a person to reflect on an incident

Consider how a person who has a learning disability or autism may feel when they have returned to a calm state following a situation in which they did not feel in control of their emotions. It is possible that many people will not understand the feelings they have experienced or the effect of their actions on others. This could be made worse if the person has difficulty in expressing themselves or if they have difficulties with communicating or understanding what is said to them. People may need time, support and help to:

- make sense of the situation;

- understand their own feelings;

- communicate how they feel about the situation;

- understand how their behaviour has affected other people around them;

- think about how they behaved and learn from the situation;

- be supported to think about how they could be better supported in the future;

- avoid getting into a situation where they feel they have no other option than to 'show how they feel' through their risky behaviour.

Your role, and the role of the team supporting the person, is to help them to understand:

- how they were feeling at the time;
- the behaviour they exhibited;
- the consequence of the behaviour;
- how they felt after the incident.

It can be difficult to discuss feelings after an incident if you support a person who has limited communication or someone who finds it hard to understand the emotions of others. This is where your detailed understanding of the person and their needs will be invaluable. Knowing about the person's autism or their hearing loss and their use of sign language will help you to determine the best course of action. It can also be useful to consider how people can express their emotions effectively. For example, you could use art, drama, music and emotional literacy work to encourage emotional expression and regulation.

Many people may not recall or recognise how the behaviour they exhibit impacts on them or others and they may need support to help them avoid using behaviour which is challenging and risky in the future.

Approaches to support a person to understand how they were feeling following an incident

1. **Privacy** – at a time of distress some people want to be alone or just with one or two people who know them well. If a person becomes distressed in a public place or in a setting with a number of other people, it often helps to either take them to a more private place or alternatively take other people away. Afterwards, some people can feel embarrassed about their period of distress and may feel awkward about meeting others again. You may be able to help by bringing them back into a group. Remember that other people may be affected by seeing someone they know well upset or distressed and their wellbeing needs to be considered.

2. **Listening and reflecting** – people who are distressed rarely want to take part in a detailed analysis of their situation and their emotional state. However, having someone who is willing to listen to their worries and unconditionally accept them can be of great benefit. Not all of the people with a learning disability or autism that you work with will be willing or able to talk about what caused them distress. Never put pressure on people to talk about things they find upsetting. If you have concerns you should seek help from an experienced counsellor or seek a referral to a psychologist or psychiatrist. Unless you have received training in counselling, beware of becoming too deeply involved in sorting out people's emotional difficulties. You can provide a great deal of help simply by listening and being sympathetic to a person's worries and anxieties.

3. **Non verbal support** – highly distressed people often find it difficult to hear or understand complex or detailed verbal messages. Some find a reassuring hand on theirs or a pat on the shoulder comforting. Although people in emotional crisis may not hear all of what is said, the tone of voice and manner in which you communicate with them can be of considerable help. A reassuring and calm tone can be more helpful than the actual words. Although some people will find a hug or hand on the shoulder reassuring and helpful, others will be embarrassed and it may add to their distress. Any indication that the person finds physical contact difficult should be clearly seen by you as a message to stop straight away.

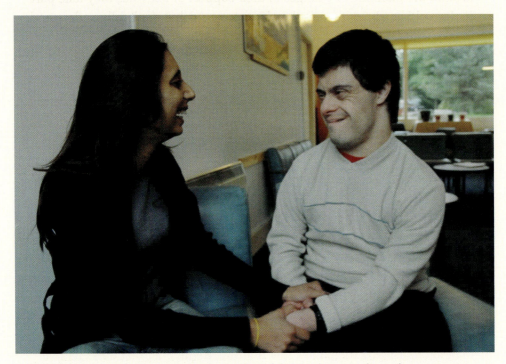

A reassuring and calm tone can be more helpful than the actual words.

4. **Physical presence** – just being there with the person in their distress following an incident is often very supportive. However, actually being physically present without doing or saying anything can be particularly difficult for some members of staff. Your knowledge of the person and their situation will help you in being with them. Some people might be happy for you to sit with them. If the person shows signs of embarrassment or of being trapped or inhibited, then it is time to consider more active support for them.

5. **Coping strategies** – learning ways of dealing with the emotions that can lead to challenging behaviour and of caring for yourself are important skills in managing incidents. Coping strategies can include relatively simple

techniques such as breathing deeply or a number of relaxation techniques. These would obviously need to be learnt before an incident happened, but can then be useful in a number of demanding or stressful situations.

6. **Information** – incidents can be caused or worsened by a lack of information, which then causes uncertainty, or when people are kept in the dark about issues that concern them. For example, colleagues or family carers may think it is in the person's best interest to know nothing about the serious illness of a relative or friend, the closure of a day service or the extent of a person's illness. The information a person might need could be around the planning of changes in their support or activities they take part in. It could be about choices they have to make, but don't fully understand.

   Not giving the person important information, for whatever reason, deprives them of using their coping skills and prevents them from making plans and choices for themselves. Giving people information when they are distressed, for example after bereavement, requires considerable skill. You should not undertake this alone, but you should involve others such as family members, colleagues, and the person's advocate, as appropriate. If the information is highly significant to that person then detailed discussion and planning may need to go on before the information is shared with the person.

7. **Relaxation and rest** – periods of stress and distress can build up a lot of tension and anxiety in the person involved. Finding ways to relieve the tension and bring about a feeling of calm and relaxation can be an important way of helping the person deal with their stress. Some people find physical activity such as swimming, walking or playing a particular sport is a good way of relieving stress. Exercise uses up the adrenaline and other hormones that build up in our bodies in times of distress and can bring about feelings of wellbeing and relaxation. Other people relax by listening to music or taking part in craft activities or other hobbies. Some people find being with or caring for animals helpful at times of distress. If you know the person you support well then you will know the things they enjoy and get pleasure from which will help them relax.

   Many people find relaxation exercise and alternative therapies useful. This could include yoga, aromatherapy or massage. These could be offered and considered by the person and those involved in their support.

8. **Lifestyle changes** – on occasions, an incident can happen in response to a number of changes in a person's daily life occurring at the same time. This can cause challenging behaviour because of the loss of predictability in their

life. It can often take a final change to tip the balance from coping to distress. In such a situation you need to investigate not only the final change that tipped the balance, but all of the issues that may have contributed to it.

Lifestyle changes for people may mean reviewing key areas such as where the person lives, how they spend their day, their friendships and leisure time. This would obviously be done over a period of time and fully involve the individual and other significant people in their life. Making changes in your own lifestyle are not usually taken lightly or hastily, but usually after careful consideration and weighing up of alternatives. You need to bear in mind the potential stress and distress that changes in lifestyle can bring in their own right, even when they are carefully planned for and agreed.

9. **Boosting self esteem** – an incident of challenging behaviour often affects a person most when it causes them to question their identity and previous life experiences. For example, finding out that one of your parents is seriously ill can make you question your identity as a daughter or son. The questioning of identity can be upsetting and disturbing for the person involved, and it may be difficult for people with poor communication skills to express these ideas and concerns. Finding ways to boost and reinforce a person's self esteem can help to increase their confidence and confirm their identity and value.

Activity

Think about a person you support and know well. Following a recent incident of challenging behaviour, which of the nine methods listed above did you use to help them return to a calm state? How effective was each of the methods you used? Are there any other ways you could support them following an incident that might help them return to a calm state? Discuss your ideas with your line manager or someone who knows the person well.

Leroy

Leroy is 26 and has limited verbal communication; Leroy has autism and a moderate learning disability. He can get very frustrated due to his communication difficulties and will rip his clothing and pull his hair out when he is upset. Leroy has been helped to overcome some of his difficulties with emotional literacy sessions supported by Della, a speech and language therapist. Della has worked closely with his family and support team to develop a personal 'story' which Leroy can use to work through his feelings.

His support staff will offer the story to Leroy when he is looking upset or after he has ripped items of clothing or pulled his hair. The story has six photos of Leroy: one taken when he was happy; one taken which shows him baking cakes (an activity he enjoys); there is a photo of him ripping clothing; one of him chatting to his mother; a photo of him chatting to his support worker; and one of him drinking a cup of Ribena (a favourite drink). It is hoped in time Leroy will seek out each photo appropriately and use it in order to get the right support at the right time.

Activity

Can you think of other things you could do to help Leroy?

How could you use the photos as part of a proactive approach?

Understanding the complex feelings of others involved in or witnessing an incident of challenging behaviour

We have already discussed the idea that people may experience a range of emotions when they are involved in an incident or witness a difficult incident. Such emotions may include:

- sadness;
- anger;
- hurt;
- fear;
- isolation;
- guilt;
- confusion.

Think about a situation which led to you experiencing one or more of the emotions above. This may be a personal experience or one related to your professional role. Think about the emotion(s) you experienced. What else did you feel? Why did you feel this way? What did you do or how did you behave as a result of how you felt? What could have helped you feel differently?

The stress associated with supporting a person who may exhibit behaviours which are of risk may lead to family members or paid workers experiencing a range of feelings:

- **Depression**: this is associated with the constant anxiety of supporting someone who presents with a range of challenges.

- **Feelings of isolation**: these can be the result of limited social experiences, poor social networks and friendships which are often inhibited by the pressure of time given to providing care for the person.

- **Feelings of inadequacy or blame**: family members or workers may believe that they cause the behaviour or that they may be making the behaviour worse.

- **Feelings of poor self esteem**: these may occur due to isolation and a decreased quality in their own relationships within the family or professional team.

- **Feelings of guilt**: these can result especially when struggling to cope and in need of additional help and support.

- **Family conflict**: family members may experience difficulties in their relationships due to the pressure of caring for a family member who has additional needs.

- **Disagreement across teams**: the pressure of supporting a person who has a high level of need may cause disagreement and lead to inconsistency in practice.

You need to be sensitive to the needs of those who support the person who is vulnerable and at risk of exhibiting challenging behaviours. Some strategies you can adopt to ensure you offer appropriate support are shown below.

Strategies for ensuring you offer appropriate support

- Ensure everyone is involved and has the opportunity to discuss their feelings and concerns, and that these will be valued and respected.

- Make sure that you and your colleagues see family carers as equal care partners. Always treat them with respect and keep them involved in the support of their family member.

- Ensure that everyone can contribute to any important decisions that affect them.

- Ensure that people have access to emotional support which is confidential – this is important for everyone affected by a person's behaviour.

- Be proactive, making sure that everyone is aware of the support systems available to them and that they can use them.

- Ensure everyone receives information and updates when appropriate. Cut out any jargon and respond to questions or requests from family members or other professionals.

- Use formal and informal opportunities for communicating with everyone.

Debriefing others involved in an incident

Debriefing describes a range of ways in which support may be offered to people who have been involved in an incident which has been difficult to manage or which has presented some challenges to respond to. It is hoped that good use of debriefing will help to lessen trauma following an unpleasant experience. The effectiveness of debriefing will vary between people. It has also been suggested that for some individuals exposure to debriefing may increase traumatic symptoms. For these reasons it is important that organisations take a responsible approach towards debriefing, given the limited research on the topic.

Ideally, a debrief or review should take place when a member of the team requests it. An incident which leads to the need to review or debrief may be one which has resulted in an injury to a person, has had an impact on how the service has been delivered, has resulted in a review of practice, or any event which is significant within the service.

Reviewing incidents is an important opportunity for learning and an opportunity to plan for the future. Whenever possible, reviews should be facilitated by someone who is not a direct member of the team involved in the incident which is being explored. The aim will be to:

- collect as much information as possible;

- identify significant contributory factors;

- highlight the approaches which were used at the time;

- highlight the actions which contributed to the incident and the outcomes;

- support everyone to make sense of the situation;

- contribute to future planning.

Review and debrief can be offered in a number of ways. A formal approach may be to record it within a one to one session or as the minutes of a meeting held by a team of staff. Debriefing can be informal when delivered immediately following an event which has caused upset or distress and is carried out in the hope of relieving the initial impact of the event and the feelings experienced by those involved.

Gibbs reflective cycle

There are a number of models and approaches which could be used to develop a formalised debrief approach. One such model is Gibbs' reflective cycle (1988). This is explained below and offers an easily understood framework.

Description
What happened?

Feelings
What were you thinking and feeling?

Evaluation
What was good and bad about the experience?

Analysis
What sense can you make of the situation?

Conclusion
What else could you have done?

Action plan
If it arose again what would you do?

1. Description

Describe the facts of what happened during the incident or episode for reflection.

2. Feelings

What were you thinking and feeling at the time? What were others telling you (if anything) about how they were thinking or feeling at the time? What were the behaviours you observed in other people? What can you recall of your own actions?

3. Evaluation

Think about what went well throughout the experience. Try and think about how things could have been better, what didn't 'go well'.

4. Analysis

What sense can you make out of the situation? Why do you think the person or others behaved as they did? Why did you behave as you did? What might have been done differently?

5. Conclusion

If you had been able to do something in a different way, what might have happened as a result? What should you perhaps not have done? How could you have averted any undesirable outcomes?

6. Action plan

Develop and agree a plan so that you can learn from this debrief process. Ensure that behaviour support plans and risk assessments are updated accordingly and record your evaluation of the event.

The above model or approach can be used as a process by a team to debrief following an incident when they have been presented with behaviours which are of risk or cause them concern. Use the story of Leonard, below, to think about how you may be able to apply this model in practice.

You can find out more about reflective practice and Gibbs' reflective cycle in the book by Lesley Barcham, *Personal Development for Learning Disability Workers* (2011), which is in this series.

Activity

Read Leonard's story, then use the six stages of the reflective cycle to evaluate the situation. Do you think using the reflective cycle could help you and the people you work with in terms of effective debriefing?

Leonard

You and a colleague have been supporting Leonard for three years and have a good understanding of him. You have been supporting him to attend a music session at the local college over the past term and he has recently asked to continue his sessions for a second term. Leonard appears to enjoy his music sessions and has made friends with a number of other people who attend. Leonard is 33; he is described as having a severe learning disability and autism.

Today you and your colleague are supporting Leonard to attend the music session. On the journey to the college Leonard is laughing about his weekend and talking about how his brother had fallen over when they were walking the family dog in the local park. His mood is happy and he is very chatty.

On arrival at the college you cannot find a parking space, which means you have to park off the college site. When you drive out of the college car park Leonard starts to ask why you're not parking at the college. You calmly explain that you have not been able to find a parking space and Leonard shouts loudly, 'Go back! Go back!'. Once again you try to repeat that there are no parking spaces and that you know where you will be able to park close by so that he will not miss his session. Leonard starts to bang his head on the car window and bite his hand. You become concerned, so you pull the car over into a safe position to try and calm Leonard. Your colleague who is sitting next to Leonard gets out of the car and you both stand on either side of the rear seats with the doors open trying to calm Leonard. He is shouting and swearing at both of you and accusing you of trying to take him home instead of taking him to attend his music session. With no warning, Leonard grabs the car door and shuts it briskly while demanding to be taken back to college. In doing so he traps your jacket in the car door pulling you off balance. Your colleague comes to your aid and Leonard gets out of the other passenger door and runs back towards the college.

You manage to get free but Leonard continues running and doesn't respond to your calls for him to stop. A passer-by sees the situation and blocks Leonard's path, allowing you time to catch up with him. You and your colleague manage to calm him and walk him to college. Leonard quickly calms when he sees the college. You support him to the music room and he attends the session without any problems.

Personal Support

We all vary in relation to the type of support we prefer. Many people will use their family and friends for informal support and this can be invaluable as it happens within existing relationships of mutual trust. It is important to remember that confidentiality should be maintained at all times and this can sometimes make informal support systems difficult to use. Organisations will offer individual supervision or one to one sessions for employees. This enables support to be available within the bounds of confidentiality. Supervision that is delivered in a supportive environment can provide a good opportunity to discuss issues and make plans for the future.

Some people prefer the anonymity of a professional counselling situation or relationship. This can be beneficial to some people and many organisations will offer such counselling support or it may be accessed through occupational health services.

Teams who support people who may use behaviours which present a risk to themselves or others will need ongoing support. Support needs will vary from person to person but there are benefits to organisations in offering good support to their employees.

Good team work involves communicating openly and honestly.

Additionally, good team work will act as a protecting factor, sometimes called a resilience factor, for individuals and teams who support people who have challenging behaviour. Good team work happens when members:

- support each other and recognise signs of stress in each other;
- communicate openly, honestly and effectively;
- share their skills and knowledge freely;
- work to an agreed or shared set of values, principles and goals;
- reflect on their practice and are active in evaluating their own practice.

Offering support and checking for injuries following an incident of challenging behaviour

It can be extremely distressing for everyone who is involved in an incident where people have been upset, frightened or hurt, including the person who may have exhibited a behaviour which is challenging. People may need support to:

1. recall the incident and their personal thoughts and feelings about it;
2. express their feelings, listen actively and respond empathetically to the feelings of other people.

As well as taking into account the need for debriefing, it is important to consider that people may have been physically injured in an incident. It is important to know how to respond to injuries which occur either to the person you are supporting, staff members, family carers or other people. Injuries may be serious and require immediate medical help which may include the need to call for an ambulance. In such instances you will need to follow the policies and procedures of your organisation.

It is more likely that people will suffer less serious injuries that do not require immediate, expert medical advice. You will need to be careful that you only check that people are well when it is safe to do so, as you could risk being injured yourself if you approach someone while they still feel cross or angry. You should also consider the person's history and who may be the best person to check them for any possible injuries.

When checking for injuries it is important to consider the following:

- Has the person calmed enough for you to have close contact with them?

- Are there obvious signs of serious injury which require immediate medical attention? In this case you must call for an ambulance or follow local policies and procedures.

- Can you deal with this as a minor injury and if so who is best to support the person? Think about who has a good relationship with the person as you don't want to risk inflaming the situation or re-triggering their behaviour.

- What is the person's history when administering first aid: are there factors such as physical or sexual abuse which might cause them to be distressed further by intimate contact at this time? Even given that it is appropriate and in the person's 'best interests', if the injury is minor you may need to delay treatment until they are calmer.

Make sure you have checked the person for any injuries which may be less obvious, as it can be easy for people to hurt themselves during crisis. They may not feel any sense of pain due to the increased levels of endorphins as a result of their heightened state of arousal.

Key points from this chapter

- It is normal for us to experience a range of feelings when presented with a challenging incident. It is how you deal with those feelings which is important.

- You have to balance your own feelings with the feelings and emotional reaction of others. This may be colleagues, and the person we are supporting, as well as their families or friends.

- You can support people to reflect on their experience and gain useful understanding of their own behaviour. The approaches that you can use include giving the person privacy, listening to their concerns, non verbal support and helping them to develop coping strategies.

- It is important to consider your own feelings and responses – to know when you might need further support and help and where you can get support if necessary.

- Debriefing and supervision is important within organisations where workers are supporting people who have complex needs. This is especially important when people are expected to manage crisis situations that present a level of risk to themselves or other people.

- Being a reflective worker can help you to understand and learn from incidents of challenging behaviour.

- People with learning disabilities and people with autism often need support to cope with stressful experiences and the distress they experience as a result.

References and where to go for more information

References

Barcham, L (2011) *Personal Development for Learning Disability Workers.* Exeter: Learning Matters/BILD

Hatton, S and Boughton, T (2011) *An Introduction to Supporting People with Autistic Spectrum Conditions.* Exeter: Learning Matters/BILD

Chapter 5

Reviewing and revising approaches to promoting positive behaviour

Parmajit's care team held a best interest meeting, in line with the requirements of the Mental Capacity Act (2005). It was agreed that it was in his best interest to use restrictive physical interventions as part of a behaviour management plan, due to the assessed risk his behaviour presented to him. Incidents have decreased dramatically due to the introduction of more person centred approaches to his support and a behaviour support plan aimed at ensuring that staff use preventative strategies. Parmajit still presents severe behavioural challenges from time to time. The use of any restrictive physical interventions is reviewed every six weeks as part of Parmajit's behaviour management plan, and is reviewed more often if there are any difficulties. When necessary, the positive behaviour support plan and the reactive management strategies (physical interventions) for responding to Parmajit's challenging behaviours are modified. In addition to recording incidents of challenging behaviour, the team is expected to record events associated with Parmajit being calm and cooperative. This information is used to develop and update the behaviour management plan to address his risky behaviours.

By keeping a record of the activities that Parmajit enjoys and participates in, staff can then offer the activities he finds most rewarding on a more frequent basis. These activities will then support Parmajit to engage in positive behaviours, offering him a worthwhile alternative to the behaviours which are regarded as challenging by others. This approach has been successful in reducing the number of incidents associated with his risky behaviours and enabling a reduction in the use of physical interventions. In time, it is anticipated that Parmajit will no longer require a reactive management plan (physical interventions).

Parmajit, his parents, and the team supporting him regularly contribute to the reviews of his support and they are kept informed of any changes to his support plan by his support worker and the team leader of the service.

Adapted from Harris et al (2008) Physical Interventions. A Policy Framework, *page 76.*

Introduction

We often try to understand and change a person's behaviour to reduce the occurrence of a behaviour which is seen as presenting a risk or a challenge; and also to encourage behaviour which is less risky and seen as more socially acceptable. Although this is not an easy task, the more we know about a person's behaviour, then the more successful we are likely to be when we try to change it. For example, you may want to know whether certain actions are more likely to occur in certain situations or when particular people are present. Direct observation and good record keeping can help to provide this information. Good observation, record keeping and a review of specific approaches are very important. If you put a lot of time, effort and resources into helping a person, then you need to know whether your hard work has paid off and you are making a positive difference to their life. Unless you are prepared to put the time and effort into observation, record keeping, reflecting and reviewing, you may never know whether or not you are making any difference.

It is important to regularly review and revise the support that is provided to a person with a learning disability or a person with autism, particularly in relation to behaviour management and the use of any physical interventions. This will ensure that the support provided reflects the person's current needs and interests, state of health and any identified risks. This chapter focuses on how to analyse information about an incident from records and reports. It then explores how good team and partnership working can contribute to reviewing records and debriefing. Finally this chapter explores how reflecting on your own involvement in an incident of challenging behaviour can contribute to promoting positive behaviour support.

Learning outcomes

This chapter will help you to:

- work with others to analyse the antecedents, behaviour and consequences of an incident of challenging behaviour;

- work with others to review the approaches to promoting positive behaviour using information from records, debriefing and support activities;

- reflect on your own role and involvement in an incident of challenging behaviour;

- consider how you can promote positive behaviour.

Working with others to analyse the antecedents, behaviour and consequences of an incident of challenging behaviour

Thinking point

Reflect on a person you support and a recent incident of challenging behaviour that you were involved in managing. Can you remember the antecedents, behaviour and consequences? How did you record this information? How was it analysed? Who was involved in recording, analysing and taking any agreed actions?

It is important to document, analyse and review incidents so that we can learn from them. A formal, structured approach to recording and examining the information gathered about incidents of challenging behaviour can provide essential evidence to inform a person's care or support plan and also their behaviour support plan. Systematically recording the antecedents, behaviour and consequences of an incident of challenging behaviour is one way to learn from and reflect on what has happened.

Antecedents are the things that occur immediately before a behaviour that is of concern; for example, it may be a change in the environment or something done or said by a person. Accurately recording the behaviour of concern is also important. For example, rather than saying *Jon shouted a lot and he shoved Nathan*, it would be better to note that *Jon shouted and swore at Nathan for nearly two minutes. He stood very close to him and pushed him three times on the shoulder. The last time Nathan lost his balance and nearly fell down.*

Finally, you need to note down the consequences of the behaviour, that is what happened immediately after the behaviour of concern has taken place. In addition to noting the antecedents, behaviour and consequences, many organisations ask people to note down the setting conditions. These could be the environmental factors that could affect each individual, including noise or bright colour. Equally, it could be specific personal issues that affect an individual such as not feeling well, having a headache or having recently experienced a loss or bereavement.

Recording of antecedents, behaviour and consequences

Activity

Look at the ABC (antecedent, behaviour, consequences) chart below. How does it compare to the forms used in your organisation? What are the similarities and differences?

Roseleaf View Centre and Homes – ABC chart

Name of resident:	Harry Jones
Date and time of record:	21 March 2012 @ 7.45 pm
Name of person completing this form:	Andy Smith
Signature of person completing this form:	A Smith

Setting conditions *What was the setting in which the behaviour occurred?*	Antecedent *What happened immediately before the behaviour occurred?*	Behaviour *Describe the behaviour*	Consequences *What happened as a result of the behaviour?*
After the evening meal at about 7.10pm, Harry was relaxing in the soft lounge by the dining table. He briefly helped with some of the tidying up. He had eaten his meal quickly as he was very keen to watch the DVD he had bought earlier. I was loading the dishwasher with Georgie. Emily was helping Paul with his dessert.	Harry called out to Emily 'Watch DVD'. Emily was helping Paul with his dessert, she said 'be with you in 10 minutes'.	Harry shouted again 'Emily watch DVD!' Then he started slapping the side of his face with the flat of his right hand. He did this about 7 or 8 times really hard. His cheek was very red at the end.	Emily left Paul and ran over to Harry. She grabbed his hand and started to stoke it while talking to him in a quiet and gentle voice. She said, 'Are you alright Harry?' Paul was left waiting to finish his dessert.

Although ABC charts are commonly used as the preferred way to record incidents of challenging behaviour, there are other recording methods that can be used. These include:

- **Diaries** – new support workers are often introduced to recording by being asked to complete entries in a handover book or diary. These are intended to provide a daily summary of significant events in a person's life.

An example of a typical diary entry

TUESDAY 4th – went swimming, had a good time. Brian didn't want to get out. Watched TV, played computer games, went to bed before 10.30 pm. Brian was good today. (LD)

WEDNESDAY 5th – two staff off sick, no cover, so no one went out today. Brian was very anxious and distressed; he twirled and twirled for ages today. Brian stayed in all day, very loud, aggressive and disruptive, shouting and swearing all afternoon and evening, went to bed really late 12 midnight. (ZA)

There are problems with this kind of record keeping, because there is often no agreement about what should and shouldn't be included. Each member of staff makes their own decision about what to include and what to leave out. As a result, we don't know whether Brian shouted aggressively on Tuesday, or for how long he shouted on Wednesday. There is often a mixture of objective observation and subjective judgement. Objective observation is the recording of behaviours that can be seen and then noted down. The answers to the following questions will give objective information. How many times did Brian shout and swear at the swimming pool? For how long did Brian twirl on Wednesday?

In contrast, subjective judgements are based on casual observation and may seek to attribute feelings to a person and make personal judgements. For example, *Brian was very anxious and distressed*. The person writing the diary could objectively observe Brian twirling, but unless he had told them that he was feeling anxious this is a subjective judgement. The person writing in the diary is seeking to explain Brian's behaviour, but it is not possible to say for certain that Brian was anxious or that his anxiety leads to the behaviour.

Diaries can be improved if the people writing in them agree on a small number of specific behaviours which are important for the person. These can be written at the top of each page in the diary with a reminder about what to record, for example, **Brian's behaviour record.** *Please note down the number of times each day he shouted inappropriately, swore and the length of time he twirls round each day.*

- **Incident record sheets** – sometimes it is useful to collect information systematically about challenging behaviour linked to a person's activities during the day. This involves providing two types of information that can be collected easily using a schedule or timetable:

  - what the person was doing;

  - whether or not a specific behaviour occurred.

For example, when during the day does Brian shout aggressively and when does he twirl and spin? By noting down on a timetable of Brian's week with an S for shouting aggressively and a T for twirling, it might be possible to identify any patterns in his behaviour.

An example of a typical incident record sheet

Week commencing 2nd March

	Morning	**Afternoon**
Sunday 2nd	walk round the lake S	Sunday lunch watch football STT
Monday 3rd	laundry and tidied room TT	cinema with brother then home T
Tuesday 4th	swimming S	in his room and computer games S TT
Wednesday 5th	keep fit cancelled SSS	weekly shop cancelled SS TT
Thursday 6th	charity shop volunteering S	walk round the lake and television TT
Friday 7th	free time TT	weekly shop then computer games TT
Saturday 8th	local shop and cafe S	football with brother SSSTT

The information provided on an incident record sheet even after a single week can provide some hints about Brian's behaviour in different settings. You would need to check that all those doing the recording were noting down the same type of behaviour. Before you analyse the information for possible patterns, you also need to ask whether you have collected information over a sufficiently long period. Then you can begin to ask what the information tells you about Brian's behaviour and whether he behaves in a similar way in similar situations.

- **Checklists** – some people present a number of different behaviours that challenge. If you are to be effective in helping them to learn other, more appropriate ways of interacting, it may be helpful to know what behaviours present a challenge and how often they occur. A simple checklist can provide a way of collecting this information. It is also important to collect information on a person's appropriate behaviours. If you only focus on behaviours that seem to challenge and ignore appropriate or positive behaviours, it is unlikely that you will be successful in supporting the person appropriately. In designing a checklist, you will need to agree what needs to be recorded with all of the people supporting the person. If there are lots of ideas, it may be necessary to focus on the most frequently mentioned or most risky behaviours that need to be addressed. Then it is important to focus on behaviours that can be objectively observed. A final method of recording needs to be agreed, such as putting a tick against each time the behaviour occurs.

A sample checklist of Brian's behaviour

MONDAY

	7–10am	10–1pm	1–4pm	4–7pm	7–10pm	TOTAL
Shouting	✓✓				✓✓✓	5
Swearing	✓✓		✓✓		✓✓✓	7
Twirling 2 mins +		✓		✓✓	✓✓✓	6
Talking quietly	✓✓✓	✓✓✓✓	✓✓	✓✓✓	✓	13
Using the trampoline 2 mins +		✓✓✓				3

Ideally this kind of checklist should be completed every day for a number of days. A full week would be useful, or possibly several days over two or three weeks. The occurrence of each behaviour can then be summarised over a period of time and possible trends identified.

Factors to consider when analysing an incident of challenging behaviour

Once reliable information has been recorded about a person and a behaviour that is challenging those who support them, it is important to consider the best way to analyse it. This analysis could be undertaken by a support worker, the manager of a service, or a professional involved in the person's care, such as a nurse, psychologist or psychiatrist. Often a multi disciplinary team is involved in the analysis of the information that is collected, and of a number of records made over a period of time.

The factors to consider in the analysis of a single incident may include the following:

- What was the person's general mood state immediately before the incident?

- Has there been any significant event in the person's life in recent weeks which may have contributed to the behaviour?

- What happened immediately before the behaviour?

- What were the immediate consequences of the behaviour for the person who exhibited it or those around them?

- What was the impact on others in the immediate environment, for example peers, workers and others who were present?

- What are the long term outcomes or consequences of the incident for the person or others affected by the incident?

It is important that once this information has been analysed, it can be used to inform the person's behaviour support plan in an appropriate way, so as to reduce the immediate risk of that behaviour occurring again.

When analysing information collected over a period of time from a number of different sources such as ABC charts, diaries and checklists, it is important to:

- check the reliability and accuracy of the data collected through discussion with those who made the records;

- summarise the information in a usable form, whether this is by using tables, graphs or other types of diagrams to give a visual representation of the records;

- check the conclusions that you draw from the information with the team of people involved in the person's support;

- use the agreed conclusions to revise the person's behaviour support plan;

- use the information collected to inform the individual behaviour risk assessment;

- appropriately engage the person and all those involved in their support about the information collected, its analysis and the conclusions drawn, and what it will mean for their ongoing support;

- ensure that the lessons learnt from the information collection and analysis are used to inform future work;

- continue to collect the information and to revise and review the behaviour support plans as appropriate.

The collection and analysis of information relating to a person's behaviour and support is an important starting point in understanding their behaviour. After information has been collected, analysed and any changes made to the person's ongoing support, it is important to continue working in partnership with all those involved to promote positive behaviour.

Working with others to review approaches to promoting positive behaviour

Thinking point

Think about a person that you support. How many other people are also involved in providing day to day support to that person? Or in supporting that person, in relation to their behaviour?

Working in partnership with others is important if the person you support is to receive good, consistent support. Family carers and close friends are particularly important when thinking about partnership working.

it shows respect and values other people's contributions

partners can have lots of information about a person to share with others

it ensures consistency of support in different settings

Partnership working is important because:

it can help with problem solving and creative thinking

different people have different skills that contribute to good support

As a support worker, working in partnership with family carers, advocates, colleagues from your own organisation and professionals from other services means:

- involving the person in decisions which affect their support;

- sharing a commitment to providing person centred support for the person;

- being clear about the information that needs to be shared, when it should be shared and with whom;

- being clear about many decisions that are made and the reasons for them;

- sharing information promptly and contributing to the analysis of information from different sources;

- learning about and respecting other people's roles and responsibilities;

- taking account of opinions and ideas that are different from your own;

- recognising that you are a member of a team of people with different strengths and talents.

Working with others to analyse and review information relating to positive behaviour support should include collating information about the incident from a variety of sources. Information can come from day to day records, ABC charts, diaries, checklists, notes from a debrief or team meetings. It can be used to:

- find out what led to the behaviour the person exhibited;

- identify triggers and any other contributory factors which increase the risk to the person or others; for example, environmental or personal conditions and external triggers;

- understand the strategies which were used and if any alternatives could or should have been tried;

- develop or modify the person's positive behaviour support plan based on the learning from this experience, which will prevent a similar situation occurring in the future;

- review written support plans, ensuring that they are still appropriate and updating them when necessary;

- review associated behavioural risk assessments and record the rationale for any strategies (which is particularly important if a planned reactive management strategy or restrictive physical intervention is part of the overall support plan to be used in an emergency situation);

- identify any changes in the person's circumstances which would indicate that there should be additional reviews or help sought; for example, the person may have health issues which would benefit from a review.

As far as is practically possible, the person should be involved in determining their support and care alongside other people in their life, such as family, advocates or close friends. They should be able to

Working with others to analyse and review information relating to positive behaviour support should include collating information about the incident from a variety of sources.

participate in the decision making process and this would include taking part in reviews such as those outlined above.

An important aspect of proactive behaviour support and analysis is the risk assessment process; whenever there is a review the risk assessment should be revisited and adjusted as necessary. There must be a continuous monitoring and review of the person's behaviour, especially when physical interventions or restrictive practices are used in an emergency or as part of a planned response.

You can find out more information about risk assessment from the book *Risk in Challenging Behaviour: a good practice guide for professionals* by Sharon Powell.

Using information to promote positive behaviour

Within organisations and services, it is important that there is an organisational culture of learning from incidents of challenging behaviour, and an ongoing review of support plans to promote positive behaviour support. This can take place on several levels:

1. Senior staff in the organisation are responsible for the development of the organisation's mission statement, values, policies and guidance and also for ensuring the safety of the people they support and employees. Senior managers influence the culture of the organisation. If value is placed on openness, learning, good communication and high quality support from those in leadership, this will assist in promoting positive behaviour support.

2. Managers of a particular service are responsible for ensuring people who are being supported, their family members and the staff, understand the values, policies and procedures of the organisation. It is important that they feel confident to pass on information or to use the compliments and complaints policies. Managers have an important contribution to make in modelling good practice, gathering and analysing information gained through supervision, debriefing, and the completion of diaries, records and checklists.

3. Individual workers also have responsibilities to promote positive behaviour support by managing information about individuals in line with the organisation's values. In addition, they should follow the policies and procedures, take an active part in supervisions and debriefings, and complete records and reports that are accurate, legible and objective rather than subjective commentary.

Activity

Reread the section on debriefing in Chapter 4 and then look at your organisation's policies on supervision and debriefing following an incident. Reflect with your line manager or an experienced colleague on how information about a recent incident was gathered and analysed. How could the information be used to promote positive behaviour support?

Supervision and debriefing are important aspects of positive behaviour support.

Reflecting on your own role in an incident of challenging behaviour and improving the promotion of positive behaviour

Reread the section in Chapter 4 on Gibbs' reflective cycle.

Activity

Using the six stages in Gibbs' model of reflection, think about a recent incident of challenging behaviour that you were involved in managing.

1. *Description*

2. *Feelings*

3. *Evaluation*

4. *Analysis*

5. *Conclusion*

6. *Action plan*

Discuss the incident and think about what actually occurred. It will be helpful to reflect on what you were feeling and perhaps the feelings expressed by other people if you have this information. Reflect on the incident and how it was managed, what other options might there have been, and whether there were alternative approaches available to you which you did not try, but which may have been effective. In the final two stages of the cycle (conclusion and action plan), focus particularly on ways that you can improve the promotion of positive behaviour.

You can find out more information on reflective practice in the book by Lesley Barcham, *Personal Development for Learning Disability Workers* (2011), which is in this series.

Key points from this chapter

- It is only possible to promote positive behaviour if the team works together and encourages the person and their family or carers to be involved in their support so far as is practically possible.

- Up-to-date, accurate reporting and recording is essential to ensuring that the support being offered to an individual is in their best interests.

- Behavioural risk assessment will underpin any behaviour support plan and provide the rationale for agreed approaches.

- Adopting approaches based on reflective practice will enable individuals and team members to be proactive in analysing their approaches.

- Organisational and personal values and approaches are important when adopting and promoting positive approaches.

References and where to go for more information

References

Barcham, L (2011) *Personal Development for Learning Disability Workers.* Exeter: Learning Matters/BILD

Harris, J et al. (2008) *Physical Interventions. A Policy Framework.* Kidderminster: BILD

Powell, S (2005) *Risk in Challenging Behaviour: A good practice guide for professionals.* Kidderminster: BILD

Chapter 6

Positive behaviour support: legislation, frameworks, policies and Codes of Practice

Inappropriate use of restraint and/or medication (relating to article 8 of the European Convention on Human Rights)

We have worked with many people with a learning disability who are being inappropriately restrained through mechanical and chemical and physical restraints. Despite guidance which sets out procedures and best practice for the decision making on restraint and use of restraint we have found worrying amounts of extremely poor practice in this area. We have also found that a restraint is often used as a way of managing low staffing levels and as a first response rather than as a carefully assessed last resort…

Diana, who has a visual impairment and scoliosis, kept colliding with people and furniture and falling, resulting in injuries. The staffing levels at her home were not sufficient to support her when walking round her home so she was strapped into her wheelchair.

Volume 1, page 50, quotes from evidence to the Joint Parliamentary Committee on Human Rights

We are extremely concerned that adults with learning disabilities undergo degrading experiences in health and residential settings… The task of securing the dignity and self respect of this vulnerable group, which is central to the fulfilment of their human rights, is the responsibility of us all. The creation of a more positive human rights culture in service provision is vital to securing respect for adults with learning disabilities in need of health and social care services.

Volume 1, page 52, Joint Parliamentary Committee on Human Rights (2008) A Life Like Any Other? Human Rights of Adults with Learning Disabilities, *London: Parliament*

Introduction

Most workers do not have the time to study the laws and government guidance that relate to the work they do; many are busy just 'getting on with the job'. However, it is important to take time to learn about the legislative framework and to recognise that the laws protect the rights of the people you support and their families, and guide you in your work. The legislation, guidance and policy are helpful in providing a framework for good, positive practice that reinforces the delivery of person centred support.

Legislation and government guidance is often put in place to protect the rights of the individual in relation to confidentiality, data protection, health and safety or in protecting people from the inappropriate use of restraint that violates their human rights. By having an increased awareness of the legislation, guidance and policy, you can ensure that you are working within the law and are addressing the principles of best practice.

This chapter will give you an overview of some of the key laws and policy documents relating to the support of people with a learning disability and people with autism. It will also outline how the relevant codes of practice should influence your support for people whose behaviour is seen to challenge services. This chapter also explains when restrictive physical interventions may be used and how to reduce their use. In addition, the chapter emphasises that the least restrictive intervention should always be used and identifies the safeguards that need to be put in place to prevent abuse.

Learning outcomes

This chapter will help you to:

- identify the legislative frameworks, guidance and codes of practice which may influence local policy and practice;

- define restrictive interventions and discuss how to reduce their use;

- explain when restrictive physical interventions may and may not be used;

- explain why the least restrictive interventions should always be used when dealing with incidents of challenging behaviour;

- describe the safeguards that must be in place when restrictive physical interventions are used.

Legislative frameworks, guidance and codes of practice which may influence local policy and practice

Health and social care practice is regulated by legislative and ethical frameworks. When considering how you will support someone (especially if you are considering the use of any restrictive practice) it is important you make decisions within an ethical, moral and legislative framework. This is important as you must always deliver care in the best interests of the people you support. Having an awareness and understanding of the laws, guidance, and codes of practice is very important when making decisions about the support you provide. In your support of people with a learning disability or people with autism, you should pay careful attention to the legislative framework as you have to ensure that you do not act in breach of legislation or statutory duty.

Different types of law

Criminal law

This is set out in statutes which are issued by Acts of Parliament, or in 'common law'. If found guilty of a criminal offence, a person may be fined or imprisoned and will have a criminal record.

Civil law

Civil law may be referred to as a 'tort', or in Scotland as a 'delict'. Civil action is taken by citizens independently of the police. Civil law governs acts of conduct between individuals. It can be used when a criminal prosecution has failed and a person decides to take civil action. An example of this would be when a person has been assaulted and they take civil action to reclaim damages for the injury sustained.

Human rights law

This is set out in the European Convention on Human Rights and in the Human Rights Act 1998. It can be used to challenge the actions of public bodies such as local authorities or the state. Action cannot be taken against individuals, although courts will make reference to the principles of the Act when interpreting the law and in making legal judgements.

Statute law

This includes any Act which is passed by the UK Act of Parliament or by the Welsh Assembly government, the Scottish Parliament or the Northern Ireland Assembly. It is the expectation that organisations and individuals always act within the law.

Statutory guidance

Statutory guidance is usually issued by government departments to provide lawful advice to statutory bodies such as local authorities. As statutory guidance is issued by a government department, an organisation needs to demonstrate good cause for delivering a service without reference to the relevant statutory guidance.

Non statutory guidance

This is most often issued by government departments to provide strong advice with reference to specific topics. There is no legal duty to follow non statutory guidance. However, local authorities may need to demonstrate a good reason for acting outside of the advice laid out within non statutory guidance.

Local policy

Health and social care providers should develop their own policies and procedures referring to existing laws and guidance. Local policy should make use of the relevant statutory and non statutory guidance. Local policies should also reflect the organisation's needs, values and mission statement and be reviewed annually.

Activity

Look at three policies from your organisation that relate to positive behaviour support. This could include the policies on behaviour support, the use of physical interventions, mental capacity or safeguarding.

Read each policy and note down any references to the current legislation or guidance. If you are unsure about the laws or guidance which relate to the policy, ask your line manager.

Legislation and codes of practice for the UK

The legislation and guidance relating to health and social care is different in England, Northern Ireland, Scotland and Wales. It is important that you are aware of the legislative requirements in the country where you work. The information provided below is not exhaustive. It provides examples of the legislation and guidance that you should be aware of and understand. For a full, up-to-date list of the appropriate legislation and guidance, you will need to ask your manager and refer to the policies and procedures of your organisation.

Human Rights Act 1998 (applies to all of the UK)

This brings into UK law the European Convention on Human Rights. When giving consideration to restrictive practices, many of the articles are relevant and should be considered, including articles 2, 3, 5, 8, 10, 14 and 17.

There is more information about the Human Rights Act in the book by Rorie Fulton and Kate Richardson, *Equality and Inclusion for Learning Disability Workers* (2011) in this series.

The Code of Practice for Social Care Workers

Alongside your responsibilities towards the people you support and the organisation that employs you, you also have wider responsibilities as one of over one million social care workers in the UK. The social care councils for each of the four countries of the UK were set up by the government in 2001 to register and regulate all social care workers. The General Social Care Council, the Care Council for Wales, The Northern Ireland Social Care Council and the Scottish Social Services Council all published *Codes of Practice for Social Care Workers* in 2002.

You should always work to the standards set out in the *Code of Practice*. They set out the standards relating to the professional conduct and practice that are required of social care workers. You will find that many of these are similar to those expected by your own organisation. However, these are set at a national level and have been devised to ensure that people who are supported and their families, carers and other members of the public know the standards of conduct they should expect from social care workers.

In relation to your responsibilities as a support worker, the Code says '... workers must strive to establish and maintain the trust and confidence of service users and carers'. This includes:

- being honest and trustworthy;

- communicating in an appropriate, open, accurate and straightforward way;

- respecting confidential information ...;

- being reliable and dependable;

- honouring work commitments ... and when it is not possible to do so, explaining why to service users and carers;

- declaring issues that might create a conflict of interest ...;

- adhering to policies and procedures about accepting gifts and money ...

The Code of Practice also says that you must not:

- exploit service users, carers and colleagues;

- form inappropriate personal relationships with service users.

For more information about the Code of Practice, see the reference section at the end of this chapter.

BILD Code of Practice for the use and reduction of restrictive physical interventions (2010)

This Code of Practice provides a voluntary framework for trainers and commissioners of training in physical interventions. The primary aim of the Code of Practice is to set common standards against which to measure training that includes physical interventions skills. It is anticipated that the application of the Code will:

- increase the emphasis on proactive and preventive approaches when supporting people who use behaviours which may be challenging;

- ensure the appropriate use of resources through the identification of risk within services;

- support the development of policy frameworks within services;

- balance the rights and responsibilities of individual staff members and individuals;

- increase awareness of the relevant legislation;

- support training organisations and commissioners of training to agree on the structure, content and frequency of such training.

The overarching aim of the Code is to emphasise the importance of restraint reduction within services. In addition, the standards outlined within the Code are used as the assessment criteria for accrediting training in physical skills in line with the BILD Physical Interventions Accreditation Scheme.

Legislative and policy framework in England

Legislation

- **Mental Capacity Act 2005**: this Act provides a statutory framework to enable decision making and assumes that all adults have the capacity to make their own decisions in relation to care or treatment unless it can be shown to be otherwise.

- **Mental Health Act 1983**: section 127 of the Act makes it an offence for an individual to 'wilfully neglect a mentally disordered person'.

- **Deprivation of Liberty Safeguards 2007**: these safeguards were implemented with amendments to both the Mental Capacity Act 2005 and the Mental Health Act 1983. They are intended to protect the rights of people who are not able to give informed consent and for whom the deprivation is found to be in their best interests.

- **Human Rights Act 1998**: UK wide legislation.

- **Autism Act 2009 (England)**: the Act's two key provisions are that an autism strategy be produced by April 2010 and that statutory guidance is issued to local authorities and health bodies on supporting the needs of adults with autism.

Statutory guidance

- **Implementing Fulfilling and Rewarding Lives**: **Autism Strategy (2010)**: required under the Autism Act 2010.

- **Valuing People Now (2009)**: the Department for Health cross-government guidance on good support for people with a learning disability in England.

Non statutory guidance

- *Guidance for Restrictive Physical Interventions: How to provide safe services for people with learning disabilities and autistic spectrum disorder (2002)*: issued jointly by the Department of Education and Skills and Department of Health, for England only. Despite being written in 2002, this guidance remains one of the most relevant documents when exploring issues relating to the care and support of people with a learning disability or autism. The document emphasises the importance of policy frameworks, together with appropriate behaviour support and training for staff.

- *Services for People with Learning Disabilities and Challenging Behaviour or Mental Health Needs* (revised edition) 2007 by Professor Jim Mansell for the Department of Health. This best practice guidance for social services and health bodies sets out the actions that need to be taken to provide good outcomes for people with learning disabilities and people with autism who can present behaviour that challenges.

Local policies

- Local and organisational policies on behaviour support.
- Local authority and organisational safeguarding procedures and policies.
- Health and safety policies.

Legislation and guidance in Scotland

Human Rights Law

The Scotland Act requires that the Human Rights Act 1998 is adhered to within Scotland.

The Adults with Incapacity (Scotland) Act 2000

This provides a framework to help safeguard the welfare and finances of people who lack capacity. It protects adults aged 16 or over who lack the capacity to take some or all decisions for themselves because of a mental disorder or an inability to communicate. In some circumstances it allows a person – such as a relative, friend or partner – to make decisions on someone's behalf. This Act discusses decisions about property, finances and welfare.

Mental Health (Care and Treatment) Scotland Act 2003

This Act contains specific guidance on the use of force. This guidance discusses the use of advance directives which may be used to engage people in decision making about the use of restrictive interventions. The Act indicates that the use of force is only permissible for as long as necessary in the circumstances.

Rights, Risks, and Limits to Freedoms 2006

Produced by the Mental Welfare Commission for Scotland, this sets out the good practice principles that should be taken into account when considering the use of restrictive practices in adult residential settings. The framework discusses the use of restraint as a 'last resort' and also stresses the need to comply with the law in delivering care and when considering the use of restraint.

Adult Support and Protection (Scotland) Act 2007

The purpose of the law is to protect people at risk from being harmed. Not everyone who is disabled is vulnerable, and the Act says that local authorities must listen to and consider the views of the adult at all times.

The Same as You? A review of services for people with learning disabilities (2000)

The Scottish Executive's statutory guidance relating to the support of people with a learning disability.

Scottish Strategy for Autism 2011

The Scottish Executive's statutory guidance relating to support for people with autistic spectrum condition.

Legislation and guidance in Wales

Framework for Physical Intervention Policy and Practice 2005

Issued by the Welsh Assembly Government as a consultation document, this sets out a framework for the use of restrictive practices including physical interventions. It is written with reference to social care, health and educational settings. In 2010, separate guidance on the use of force in schools was issued in Wales entitled *Safe and Effective Intervention: Use of reasonable force and searching for weapons.*

The Mental Capacity Act 2005

This Act applies in Wales. It provides a clearer legal basis for making decisions and in doing so promotes best practice in supporting people who may lack mental capacity. The Act sets out in law what happens when people are unable to make decisions.

Human Rights Act 1998

This Act applies in Wales.

The Statement on Policy and Practice for Adults with a Learning Disability (2007)

This is a report to the National Assembly of Wales on services for people with a learning disability. The policy covers key areas of advocacy, person centred planning, transition, day opportunities, employment and housing.

The Autistic Spectrum Disorder (ASD) Strategic Action Plan for Wales 2008

Guidance for local authorities in Wales on support for all people on the austistic spectrum.

Legislation and guidance in Northern Ireland

Human Rights Act 1998

This Act applies in Northern Ireland.

Mental Health (Northern Ireland) Order 1986

This order, and subsequent amendments, sets out details about the assessment and detention of people because of 'mental disorders'.

Equal Lives: Review of policy and services for people with a learning disability in Northern Ireland (2005)

The Department of Health and Social Services and Public Safety policy on support for people with a learning disability.

The Autism Act (Northern Ireland) 2011

This states that the Department of Health, Social Services and Public Safety has to prepare a strategy on autism within two years.

Local policy frameworks

An important consideration within any organisation that supports individuals whose behaviour may be seen as challenging is the development of appropriate local policies and procedures. In the book *Physical interventions. A Policy Framework* (2008) the authors propose that the building blocks for such policies should include the following four elements:

1. **Physical wellbeing**: ensuring that people have access to good healthcare and support. This should include psychological care. An important aspect of physical wellbeing is protection from bullying and/or abuse or exploitation. There should be good policy frameworks to support individuals to make complaints when they arise.

2. **Emotional wellbeing**: this includes supporting people to engage in meaningful activities, maintaining a range of friendships and having the opportunity to develop new friendships. It is important that people are supported to maintain contact with family members and are supported to experience a lifestyle which reflects their cultural and spiritual background and expressed needs.

3. **Material wellbeing**: people should be respected as individuals who have a right to live in comfortable surroundings with access to their personal property. Important factors that affect the day to day quality of a person's life include how they spend their money, where they spend it, and what they choose to do with their time.

4. **Social wellbeing:** being able to have one's own rights and choices respected and acted upon. People have the right to express their individuality through their close relationships, spirituality and self expression.

Local policies need to ensure the emotional wellbeing of people, supporting them to maintain contact with family members and friends.

Defining restrictive interventions and ways to reduce their use

This book concentrates on promoting positive behaviour support. Restrictive interventions should not be seen as part of any positive behaviour support plan. Instead, restrictive interventions are a component of a reactive management strategy. Reactive strategies are usually implemented as a last resort when other alternatives have been tried and have failed to reduce the level of arousal and risk presented by a person's behaviour.

Any person who is known to present behaviour that is of risk should have an individual behaviour support plan. This must detail the personal support plan and include primary preventative approaches, secondary preventative strategies and planned responses to use when the behaviour(s) of concern continue to escalate (these are explained in more detail in Chapter 2). In a few exceptional circumstances, this may include a planned emergency response that determines the possible use of a restrictive practice, most often physical intervention.

The term 'restrictive intervention' covers four main categories:

1. Direct physical contact between a professional and a person whom they are supporting.

   This may include holding a person who is trying to attack another person.

2. The use of barriers to limit freedom of movement. This may be simply putting a table between yourself and another person as a barrier. A more significant barrier would be closing the door to isolate someone in a room. This is sometimes called seclusion. It is important to be aware that seclusion is legally defined and cannot be implemented without a clear and lawful reason.

   This may include locking doors or using key pads to restrict any movement between living areas.

3. The use of specially designed equipment to restrict movement, most often called a mechanical restraint.

   This might include the application of arm splints or a lap strap on a chair, seat or wheelchair.

4. The use of medication. This is often called chemical restraint and must be prescribed by a qualified medical practitioner.

   This may include the prescription of medication to be given when necessary to help a person manage their behaviour.

When discussing restrictive practices, it is important to realise that in most circumstances people can be supported without implementing a planned or emergency response involving restrictive interventions. The use of any restrictive practice should be clearly set out as written guidance within service policies.

This chapter has been written referring to the use of restrictive physical interventions; however, many of the principles discussed apply when implementing any form of restrictive practice. Good practice principles include the development and implementation of:

- service guidance and protocols for implementing individual behaviour support plans, aimed at preventing behaviours that challenge by offering alternatives to the person;

- service guidance relevant to positive behaviour support;

- service guidance and protocols relevant to the use of restrictive practices;

- robust behaviour assessments which have been well documented;

- behaviour risk assessment, and ensuring that there are positive approaches towards managing risk;

- current risk assessment for those individuals who present behaviours of risk, and ensuring that these are reviewed on a regular basis;

- clear guidance for consulting with the person receiving the support, and including them in any decision making process that relates to their care or treatment wherever possible;

- a clear process for consulting with relevant other people, such as family carers, advocates and friends where appropriate;

- a written protocol which has been agreed on capacity, decision making and consent (this must be done with reference to appropriate legislative requirements including the Mental Capacity Act (2005));

- regular reviews of any individual support plan that includes a response which could be viewed as a restrictive practice.

Good practice principles include having a clear process for consulting the person involved and their family carers.

Always use the least restrictive interventions

When deciding to implement any restrictive practice in response to an incident of challenging behaviour, it is important that it must be the least restrictive option available to you. This means that you should:

- consider and implement all reasonable options that are available to you before you use a restrictive intervention;

- ensure that you implement an approach that is the least restrictive in order to reduce the presenting risk;

- consider how much risk is presented by the behaviour when deciding on the most effective approach to reducing that risk;

- only implement any restrictive interventions when absolutely necessary, and only for as long as is absolutely necessary;

- ensure that the support you are offering the person is in their best interests within the framework of the Mental Capacity Act 2005 (England and Wales) or the relevant capacity legislation for the country you work in;

- never use a physical or any restrictive intervention to punish a person or as a consequence of a behaviour;

- never consider the use of physical interventions which relies on the application of pain to the person or use such a technique to gain compliance from the person;

- consider any contraindications for the use of physical interventions; for example, does the person have a medical condition which may give rise to concern or which might increase the risk to them if they are held?

Activity

Have a look at an existing support plan which includes strategies for using a physical intervention as a last resort; this is often called a planned response. Think about the following factors when considering this plan:

- *Has the person, and the people who are important to them, been included in developing this plan?*

- *Is there an accessible version of the person's support plan that they can have access to and that is easily understood by them?*

- *Is there a risk assessment which is well documented and relates to the management plan? Are the risk reduction strategies well documented and are they easily understood by support workers and other professionals involved in supporting the person?*

- *Are there positive and proactive behaviour support strategies in place which offer the person alternatives to exhibiting behaviours that are considered to be 'risky' and which may lead to the use of a restrictive intervention being employed? Does the person have a positive behaviour support plan and is this accessible and easily understood by the person and those people supporting them?*

- *If the plan includes the use of restraint or other restrictive practices, what alternatives have been considered? Why would the alternatives not work and might there be an opportunity to reconsider the use of some alternative strategies in the future? If this is an option, what would indicate that we should consider an alternative or when might the plan be reviewed?*

- *If restraint is used, it must be at the minimum level and for the shortest time possible to reduce the level of risk to the most acceptable level. It should never be used to punish the person nor should restraint be used as a consequence for behaviour. The use of restraint must always be with the aim of reducing the immediate risk to the person or others or if the person is in danger of committing an offence. Has the plan explained how to ensure that the use of restraint is in the person's best interest, with reference to the relevant legislation on capacity, and complies with the principles of minimum force?*

- *Does the plan enable the professionals supporting the person to review the strategies on a regular basis? Are there adequate opportunities to record and review the actions of the team and ensure that best practice principles are being applied?*

- *Is there a restraint reduction plan in place? If there is, is it easily understood, can it be reviewed regularly and is there opportunity to implement restraint reduction strategies?*

- *Where there are planned responses in place, is it possible to undertake an audit of the strategies across a service? Would you know when restraint is used, on whom it is used, what type of restraint it is and for how long it was implemented?*

In thinking about the above principles, you will be starting to consider some of the best practice principles which will contribute to restraint reduction within your service. In turn, this will increase reliance on positive behaviour support plans.

Safeguards that must be in place if a restrictive physical intervention is used

Undertaking risk assessments when supporting a person who has behaviours which are of concern is important in order to demonstrate compliance with good practice principles and legislative requirements. This is very important when you may have to implement the use of restrictive practices as a last resort.

This risk assessment should include:

- the identification of the environments, activities or personal setting conditions/factors which may give rise to or increase risk for the individual;

- an assessment of the likelihood of the behaviour and the severity of the outcomes associated with the behaviour;

- identification of the potential consequences of such outcomes and who will be affected by them;

- documented evidence of all of the information relevant to the assessed risk and the actions taken to prevent and reduce risk;

- documented evidence of the regular reviews of the risk and associated behaviour support plans.

Any individual reactive management strategy which includes the planned use of a reactive strategy or intervention should be agreed by a multidisciplinary team. The use of such an intervention should be within the legislative framework and guidance outlined above. No team member or professional supporting a person who presents behaviours which are of risk should be expected to use any restrictive interventions without appropriate training and/or authorisation. Best practice means that such interventions must be specific to the individual and a particular behaviour. In all situations, there should be a plan and an individual approach that includes:

- the name of the person being supported and other relevant personal details;

- a behaviour assessment which details the behaviour(s) of concern and risk;

- a hypothesis in relation to the causes, triggers and functions of the behaviour(s);

- a risk assessment which is specific to the behavioural risk and explores the environmental setting conditions, consequences, outcomes and risk reductions strategies as discussed above;

- primary prevention strategies to defuse and de-escalate the behaviour;

- secondary strategies to implement when primary strategies are not practical or have been ineffective;

- information to help professionals recognise when the person is reaching crisis or may present a significant risk;

- details of which behaviour(s) may require a response that includes a restrictive practice;

- the description of the specific strategy which is to be implemented and the indicators which will allow the restrictive strategy to be discontinued;

- a description of the role of the team involved in supporting the person, prior to the intervention, throughout the intervention and following any incident which has included a restrictive practice;

- information on debrief strategies and options of support for the person, other people present and the professionals involved;

- a description of how any incidents should be reported, in line with the local policy and protocols, and how information should be recorded for future planning and review; of particular importance will be the link made to ongoing risk assessments.

When may restrictive physical interventions not be used?

It is important to consider when the use of physical interventions may be inappropriate.

This chapter has already highlighted the need to ensure that restrictive physical interventions are only ever implemented when there is a clearly assessed risk that indicates the need to do so, when there is no alternative to reduce the presenting risk.

It is paramount that any use of restrictive physical interventions is lawful: for example, it is not lawful to implement seclusion on a regular basis in community settings or where a person is not detained with the protection of the Mental Health Act (1983), or the relevant legislation for the country you work in. Additionally, careful consideration should be given to the following:

- What is the general health of the person? Are there any known health conditions which may give rise to any increased risk when using a restrictive physical intervention, for example epilepsy, asthma, or osteoporosis?

- Has the person had any previous trauma or experiences which may give rise to an increase in behaviour which presents a level of risk? For example, it is possible that people who have experienced significant physical or sexual abuse may re-live traumatic life events when they are exposed to the use of physical interventions;

- Is there an alternative approach which is less restrictive that will effectively gain the same or a similar outcome in reducing the level of risk to stopping the behaviour?

Reporting and recording

It is expected that organisations should set out clear guidance on reporting and recording, and section 11 of the Joint Guidance (2002) addresses this issue.

In most settings, records which are maintained are legal documents and may also be subject to the Data Protection Act (1998). Records should be maintained to a standard format and should be stored securely. Managers are expected to ensure that records are legible, appropriate, up to date, monitored on a regular basis and used to inform practice.

Good reporting and recording will ensure that the service complies with legislative requirements. Following an incident which has included the use of any physical intervention or restrictive practice, it will be important to ensure that a good record is maintained. It should include information such as who was involved in the incident, who was informed of the incident, an account of the incident and the responses used by the team. Any damage to property should be recorded, as should any injuries or treatment required by anyone as a result of the incident. It will be important to date and sign any documents for future reference.

Reporting and recording should be completed as soon as is practically possible following any incident which gives rise to a reporting process. Reporting should be accurate and should not be tampered with or amended materially in any way after completion. In most services, records will be regarded as legal documentation and will be reviewed in the event of any complaint.

Safeguarding individuals and the use of restrictive interventions

Over the years, instances of abuse within services for people who have a learning disability and people with autism have shown that the inappropriate use of physical interventions and other restrictive practices have often played a part. In recent years, these have included the BBC's *Panorama* programme, 31 May 2011, and the investigations in Cornwall (2006) and Sutton and Merton (2007).

Practices have included the inappropriate use of locked doors to prevent freedom of movement and the inappropriate use of wheelchair lap straps to stop people walking about; these are examples of practice which should be considered unlawful. Often abuse occurs within services because a culture has developed where practice is not questioned and staff and the people who use the service feel isolated and vulnerable. Good policy frameworks can go some way to developing a culture that promotes people's rights and where abuse is less likely to occur.

It is important that any restrictive practice is only used when absolutely necessary as a last resort and for the minimum amount of time necessary to achieve a decrease in the level of risk. A restrictive intervention should be a short term measure and not viewed as a long term solution to managing a person's behaviour. A positive behaviour support plan is the most appropriate way to support a person in the long term and to achieve lasting behavioural change.

Although we most often think of the physical harm that can occur as a result of using restrictive interventions, people can also experience psychological trauma. We can reduce the risks to individuals by ensuring that all of the approaches are individualised and take account of their previous experiences, any medical conditions and other personal aspects which may impact on their behaviour. Many people with autism and people with learning disabilities experience poor health and there is also some evidence that they may be at greater risk than the general population of experiencing a range of mental health problems. If a person experiences a medical condition this must be taken into account before the use of any restrictive practice.

Using the individualised approaches discussed within this book will help ensure the best interests of individuals and prevent instances of abusive practice. Individualised behaviour support approaches should be supported by good policy and practice guidelines, protocols and training for the whole staff team. In individual services, adult safeguarding policies must be given importance and these should be current and based on legislation and guidance. Training must be relevant to the working environment and challenges that staff are likely to face on a day to day basis. It is important that training is integrated across the service and adult safeguarding issues are covered within induction programmes for all staff, not just direct care staff.

For training to be effective in preventing abuse, it should be targeted towards the needs of individuals and support the staff team to understand them better. An important aspect of creating a positive culture is also ensuring that staff receive regular support and supervision enabling them to discuss any concerns they may have. Staff should have access to whistle blowing procedures and understand how to use them so that any concerns they have can be aired in confidence. The people using a service should have a forum to offer feedback to the service, and they should also be involved in the decisions that affect them. This will enable people to develop good communication skills and understanding of how to make a complaint, should the need arise.

A good practice checklist for safeguarding when considering restrictive practices

1. Are all the steps in place to effectively support the person and has their behaviour been fully assessed?

2. Is there evidence of proactive approaches to supporting the individual?

3. Do we have all the necessary medical information necessary to support the person?

4. Is the behaviour support plan well written, easily understood and are team members implementing proactive approaches in a consistent manner?

5. If restrictive practices are being considered, how can we ensure that they are used for the minimum period of time, their use is reasonable, and that there is no other alternative course of action available at this time?

6. What steps have been taken to assess and minimise the risk to the person and the professionals who are supporting them at this time?

7. How will practice be reviewed and who will take responsibility?

8. How do we plan to reduce the use of any restrictive practice?

9. Is the approach consistent with the requirement of 'best interest' as stipulated by the Mental Capacity Act (England and Wales) or the appropriate capacity legislation for the country you work in?

Activity

Frances is 33 years old and lives in a house with three other women. Frances has severe learning disabilities and limited communication. She does use signs but these are ones she has developed over time and are usually only recognised by the people who support her on a regular basis. They have all lived together for just over five years. Recently Frances was unwell and had to spend some time in hospital. On her discharge, it was reluctantly decided by the team that supports her that she should move to a downstairs bedroom as her mobility was now poorer and this would enable her to return home sooner.

Initially, Frances seemed to be happy to return home. However, after two days she started to show signs of being upset, crying for no reason and shouting at people. Staff noted these changes in her usual happy demeanour and decided they would try to reassure Frances, possibly believing that she was still feeling unwell and recognising she may be upset at the change in her living arrangements.

Three days following her discharge from hospital, Frances was more upset than she had been previously. After she had eaten breakfast, she became very loud, shouting and crying, and she then hit a support worker who went to comfort her. Staff decided to stand back, believing this may calm her. However, Frances threw a heavy book at a fellow householder, a person considered to be her friend. She then grabbed the woman by the shoulders and started to shake her. Staff felt that they had no choice but to intervene and restrain Frances to stop her hurting the other woman who was very distressed by the incident, though unhurt.

1. *Consider what may reasonably have been done to prevent this situation from developing.*

2. *Do you believe the staff acted reasonably in implementing a physical restraint? What should they have considered?*

3. *Discuss the relevant legislative frameworks and guidance that the team will need to consider.*

Key points from this chapter

- You have a responsibility to be aware of the legislation, guidance and local policies that directly impact on the support you provide.

- All workers are responsible and accountable for their own practice and ensuring that their practice complies with legislation and guidance.

- You need to be aware of how using legislative framework and guidance can improve the outcomes for the individuals you support.

- Ensuring that the principles of positive behaviour support are fully understood and put into practice will reduce any reliance on the use of restrictive practices.

- Good reporting and recording is at the heart of the good practice principles and will enable you to make sound judgements when evaluating the support you offer individuals.

References and where to go for more information

References

BBC (2011) *Panorama: Care – The Abuse Exposed*, broadcast on 31 May

Bickerton, S (2011) *Principles of Safeguarding and Protection for Learning Disability Workers.* Exeter: Learning Matters/BILD

BILD (2010) *BILD Code of Practice for the Use and Reduction of Restrictive Physical Interventions*, third edition. Kidderminster: BILD

Fulton, R and Richardson, K (2011) *Equality and Inclusion for Learning Disability Workers.* Exeter: Learning Matters/BILD

Hardie, E and Tilly, L (2012) *An Introduction to Supporting People with a Learning Disability.* Exeter: Learning Matters/BILD

Harris, J et al. (2008) *Physical Interventions. A Policy Framework.* Kidderminster: BILD

Lyon, C et al. (2004) *Physical Interventions and the Law.* Kidderminster: BILD

Legislation, policies and reports

All legislation can be downloaded from www.legislation.gov.uk

Policies and reports for Northern Ireland, Scotland and Wales can be found at: www.northernireland.gov.uk www.scotland.gov.uk and www.wales.gov.uk Policies and reports for England can be found on the website of the relevant government department.

Joint Parliamentary Committee on Human Rights (2008) *A Life Like Any Other? Human rights of adults with learning disabilities.* London: The Stationery Office

Healthcare Commission and CSCI (2006) *Joint Investigation into the Provision of Services for People with Learning Disabilities at Cornwall Partnership NHS Trust.* London: Healthcare Commission and CSCI

Healthcare Commission (2007) *Investigation into the Service for People with Learning Disabilities provided by Sutton and Merton Primary Care Trust.* London: Healthcare Commission

Key legislation and guidance in England

Autism Act 2009

Data Protection Act 1998

Deprivation of Liberty Safeguards 2007

Human Rights Act 1998

Mental Capacity Act 2005

Mental Health Act 1983

Department of Health and Department for Education and Skills (2002) *Guidance for Restrictive Physical Interventions: How to provide safe services for people with learning disabilities and autistic spectrum disorder* . London: DH and DfES

Department of Health (2009) *Valuing People Now: A new three-year strategy for people with learning disabilities.* London: Department of Health

Department of Health (2010) *Implementing Fulfilling and Rewarding Lives: Statutory guidance for local authorities and NHS organisations to support implementation of the autism strategy.* London: Department of Health

Key legislation and guidance in Northern Ireland

The Autism Act (Northern Ireland) 2011

Human Rights Act 1998

Mental Health (Northern Ireland) Order 1986

The Department of Health, Social Services and Public Safety (2005) *Equal Lives: Review of policy and services for people with a learning disability in Northern Ireland.* Belfast: DHSSPSNI

Key legislation and guidance in Scotland

Human Rights Act 1998

The Adults with Incapacity (Scotland) Act 2000

Mental Health (care and treatment) Scotland Act 2003

Rights, Risks and Limits to Freedoms 2006

Adult Support and Protection (Scotland) Act 2007

Scottish Strategy for Autism 2011

Scottish Executive (2000) *The Same as You? A review of services for people with learning disabilities.* Edinburgh: Scottish Executive

Key legislation and guidance in Wales

The Autistic Spectrum Disorder (ASD) Strategic Action Plan for Wales 2008

Human Rights Act 1998

Mental Capacity Act 2005

Welsh Assembly Government (2005) *Framework for Restrictive Physical Interventions Policy and Practice.* Cardiff: Welsh Assembly Government

Welsh Assembly Government (2007) *Statement on Policy and Practice for Adults with a Learning Disability.* Cardiff: Welsh Assembly Government

Further information

Codes of Practice for Social Care Workers (2002) for England, Northern Ireland, Scotland and Wales are available from:

> **General Social Care Council (England)**
> Skipton House, 80 London Road, London, SE1 6LH
> 020 7397 5100 www.gscc.org.uk

> **Care Council for Wales**
> South Gate House, Wood Street, Cardiff CF10 1EW
> 0300 30 33 444 www.ccwales.org.uk

> **Scottish Social Services Council**
> Compass House, 11 Riverside Drive
> Dundee, DD1 4NY
> 0845 60 30 891 www.sssc.uk.com

> **Northern Ireland Social Care Council**
> 7th Floor, Millennium House, 19–25 Great Victoria Street
> Belfast BT2 7AQ
> 028 9041 7600 www.niscc.info

Glossary

Abuse – a violation of a person's human and civil rights by any other person or persons, which usually involves a misuse of power.

Antecedents – something that occurs immediately before a behaviour, for example it may be a change in the environment or something done or said by a person.

Advocacy – helping and supporting someone else to speak up for what they want.

Autistic spectrum condition – autism is a lifelong developmental disability. The word 'spectrum' is used because whilst all people with autism experience difficulties in the same areas (they all have problems with communication, social interaction, ways of thinking and sensory processing), autism affects people in a wide variety of different ways. Those most severely impacted upon by their autistic spectrum conditions can be seen as at one end of the spectrum, whilst those who are able to function easily with little or no support can be seen as being at the other end of the spectrum.

Behaviour support plan – an individualised plan which helps carers to be consistent in promoting positive behaviour. The plan will be proactive and promote alternatives to any risky behaviours.

Care plan – see Support plan.

Challenging behaviour – behaviour which puts the safety of the person or others at risk, or which has a significant impact on the quality of life of the person or other people.

Communication – the way that two or more people make contact, build relationships and share messages. These messages can be ideas, thoughts or feelings as well as information and questions. Communication involves both sending and understanding these messages and can be done through many different ways including speech, writing, drawing, pictures, symbols, signs, pointing and body language.

Consequences – the immediate outcomes of a behaviour. It is what happened immediately after the 'target behaviour' has taken place.

Debriefing – a supportive process enabling an individual or team to reflect on a particular situation or incident. Debriefing can help people understand the possible factors that influenced an incident and help them to plan effectively for the future and any reoccurrence.

De-escalate – a strategy used to reduce anxiety expressed by a person and prevent them exhibiting a more risky behaviour.

Defusing – a strategy used during an incident to calm the person and perhaps offer them an alternative to behaving in a risky way.

Environmental factors – things which are present around the person that may contribute to their behaviour or conversely be calming to them. An example of a calming environmental factor might be a fish tank or pet.

Family carer – a relative of a person with learning disabilities, or a person with autism, who has an interest in their wellbeing.

Functions of behaviour – the reasons or the purpose of a behaviour.

Functional assessment – an assessment that enables an understanding of why an individual exhibits specific behaviours.

Incident – when something occurs that is out of the ordinary and has an impact on people or the environment.

Intellectual disability – a term used increasingly in countries, such as the USA, Canada and Australia, to mean the same as the term 'learning disability' used in the UK.

Learning disability – a learning disability is an impairment that starts before adulthood and that has a lasting effect on the person's development. It includes the presence of a significantly reduced ability to understand new or complex information or to learn new skills. It also means having a reduced ability to cope independently.

Legislation – the laws that are in force that address particular issues.

Mental capacity – a person's ability to make their own decisions and to understand the consequences of those decisions.

Non statutory guidance – guidance that is issued by government departments which should be followed, but is not legally binding.

Person centred approach – a way of working every day with people with learning disabilities that puts the person and their preferences at the centre of everything you do.

Person centred planning – a structured approach to make sure that people with learning disabilities and people with autism are at the centre of all planning, choices and discussions about their life. Person centred planning helps them to live their lives in their own way and to meet their wishes and desires.

Personal factors – multiple elements that affect a specific person.

Physical interventions or physical restraint – any method of responding to challenging behaviour which involves some degree of direct physical force to limit or restrict any person's movement or mobility.

Policy – a plan or statement describing how a government or organisation will work towards their aims and objectives on a particular issue.

Positive behaviour support – a proactive structured behavioural approach aimed at reducing risky behaviours.

Primary prevention strategies – strategies which can be implemented to prevent a specific behaviour.

Proactive strategies – approaches that support a person in positive ways, seeking to address a person's needs before they need to communicate through risky behaviours. Proactive strategies provide alternatives to the risky or challenging behaviours.

Procedure – a set of instructions which sets out in detail how a policy should be implemented and what staff should do in response to a specific situation.

Reactive strategies – behaviour management strategies used when a situation presents significant risk and there are no alternatives.

Reflection – careful consideration of ideas and issues.

Restraint reduction – approaches aimed at reducing the use of a range of restrictive practices or physical interventions.

Restrictive intervention – a practice that could restrict or deprive an individual of their liberty.

Restrictive strategies – approaches implemented to reduce any given risk when there is no reasonable alternative. This may include the use of a physical intervention.

Risk – the probability or threat of damage, injury, liability, loss, or other negative occurrence which may be prevented through planned action.

Risk assessment – a careful examination of what could cause harm to people, so that you can weigh up whether you have taken enough precautions or should do more to prevent the possibility of harm.

Rights – a framework of laws that protects people from harm, sets out what people can say and do and guarantees the right to a fair trial and other basic entitlements, such as the right to respect, dignity and equality.

Safeguarding – helping to protect vulnerable people from abuse by others.

Secondary strategies – planned approaches for reducing any crisis and preventing an escalation in behaviour.

Self injury – an act of hurting oneself deliberately.

Service – the provision of social care support for a person, which could be provided in their own home, in their local community, in a residential home or any similar place.

Socially inappropriate behaviour – a behaviour that is viewed as inappropriate by other people, given the social and cultural context in which it is exhibited.

Statutory guidance – guidance which has been developed through the legislative framework and must be followed and addressed.

Support plan – a detailed plan of a person's needs that workers should use to inform their day-to-day support for that individual.

Trigger – something which will cause a sequence of events. Often the trigger is the reason why a person then exhibits a risky behaviour.

Index

Added to a page number 'g' denotes glossary.